THE EMPOWERED CHALLENGER PLAYBOOK

THE EMPOWERED CHALLENGER PLAYBOOK

HOW BRANDS CAN CHANGE THE GAME, STEAL MARKET SHARE, *and* TOPPLE GIANTS

PRENTICE HOWE

KING'S WAY PRESS

THE EMPOWERED CHALLENGER PLAYBOOK
How Brands Can Change the Game, Steal Market Share, and Topple Giants

ISBN 978-1-61961-566-3 *Paperback*
978-1-61961-567-0 *Ebook*

To Natalie, Cameron, Mars and all those who have ever said to themselves, "I think I can…I think I can…"

CONTENTS

FOREWORD

BY MICHAEL PORTMAN
CO-FOUNDER, BIRDS BARBERSHOP
CO-FOUNDER, VERB PRODUCTS

I've always been a challenger, but it took Prentice Howe to make me an empowered one. We were just out of school, living as roommates, striving to become paid creatives.

Prentice broke out early, but I waited tables for almost a year before getting an entry-level writing job. To this day, juggling all those food and drink orders while exuding cheerfulness despite the omnipresent smell of ketchup is the hardest work I've ever done. I stunk so bad that I owned the smoking section dayshift.

One day, the restaurant manager in the Tasmanian Devil tie put me on the PM schedule. After a series of spills and botched checks, he called me over to his corner booth. I recoiled and huffed throughout the sermon. “Look,” he said. “I’m just trying to prepare you for the rest of your life.”

When I finally landed a respectable copywriting gig, it felt like vindication unfulfilled. I’d never had a sufficient reply for that manager. To friends I claimed that I could only show him how prepared I was for the rest of my life in my birthday suit.

Prentice put twenty dollars on the table and told me to put it where my mouth is. He’d be the lookout, and a third conspirator would drive the getaway car.

Empowered, this challenger burst in at prime dinner hour, repeating handbook jargon throughout the restaurant as loudly as possible, nude except for a lowered hat and cowboy boots.

The Naked Run was the first domino. Had Prentice not given the push to do it, we wouldn’t have decided later that it would make a funny movie scene. Within a year we’d written a script and moved to Los Angeles.

Had I not moved to LA, I wouldn't have gotten a day job writing speeches for the president of Disneyland. Had I not gotten employed, I wouldn't have bought a home in Silverlake before it got cool. Had I not paid the most money for anything ever on housing, I would have moved closer to work. Had I moved closer, two hours a day on LA freeways wouldn't have been too much. Had the commute not been too much, I wouldn't have quit Disney with no plan but to sell the house and not buy a new one.

My wife and I traveled a year and ended up in Austin. It was time to figure out where necessities were. Haircuts came up in a conversation with another childhood friend, Jayson Rapaport. Every salon or barber shop he mentioned was either cheap and chainy or fancy and fancily priced. Getting a haircut was a chore, and he didn't have a suitable alternative. Jayson, the left brain to my right, saw something there.

The result of that conversation is Birds, a barbershop for everyone where the art is big, the arcade games old, the music curated, and cold Shiner beer is always available. Fun aside, employee satisfaction comes first, quality haircuts follow naturally, and we keep prices in check for the customer. Each location is hyper-designed to its space, each echoing its own neighborhood.

So much in this book resonates with our own journey as small business owners. Compulsive servitude and constant evolution pay the bills, but there's also our lightning-rod-like devotion to being a unisex take on an old, dudes-only idea. Heretical though it may be, we think you ought to look forward to a haircut instead of treating it like another to-do. We know some people want the cheapest buzz possible, and others want to spend the afternoon pampered in a salon. Prentice calls it "fostering rejection"; we call it not wasting time trying to convert those who aren't likely clients anyway.

The Empowered Challenger Handbook is the closest I've seen to a guide on creativity—and how to *outthink* those who will always be able to outspend. Prentice breaks the great ideas down into their parts, but even more importantly, he lends great importance to questioning the assumptions around us. Why not ban typical salon drama? Why not stay open seven days a week? Why not give customers a beer with the haircut?

The brands we love accomplish something no business before them could. They anticipate a void we didn't know existed. *The Empowered Challenger Handbook* encourages our skepticism and hones in on the distinct advantage of our own inner doldrums, encouraging us to ask: Who says our company has to appeal to every kind of woman?

Why not talk to our customers like friends? Who says a loyalty program needs to be a punch card? This book is a guide to letting minds wander with purpose to find their unique challenger-abilities.

It took a decade of building one Birds Barbershop a year, every year, to finally accept that I was a business person and not just an English major who still didn't know what EBITDA meant. Excel spreadsheets fall to Jayson, my cofounding partner who is also a walking operations manual, as I focus on words, pictures, and bricks and mortar. We question ourselves constantly, nudging one another to each next step—thoughtful nimbleness achieved in slow motion that only feels creative months or years—or maybe never—later.

Creativity is a gift to some, but learned by most of us. Many are trained to know how, when, and where, but far fewer are encouraged to invent what and feel why. Originality, by definition, can't be taught, but becoming a lightning rod for electricity to strike will up the ante. Kids, naïve, do this well. As a creative guy named Picasso once said, "Every child is an artist. The problem is staying a child as you grow up."

It's up to creative people to flip the script from being just a line item on the budget, and to make creativity the essence of the budget itself. Once an idea is set in motion, it is up to the gazillion ideas that follow to make the business adapt to its environment. It could be coordinating a timely promo tie-in with a like-minded brand, executing a waiting-room overhaul from art to install, communicating a change to walk-in procedure, or finally building that expensive geo-locating reservation app with the built-in rewards program because it's finally worth doing. Without a team of creative professionals asking the "but why" questions posed in these pages, none of us would have the skills to stay nimble through a typical workweek.

The ability to challenge is an opportunity, as Prentice writes, not a burden. Regular people can topple giants if the idea and execution are great enough. For my business partner and I, that realization came only recently after we realized that our experience made us just as equipped as anyone to make our own brand a household name, even though neither of us knows how to cut hair. We'll see how far that naïveté takes us.

At Fortune 500 companies you hear a lot about the "brain drain" of those lost to new idea factories. It's a hard flow to stem in the start-up era, and that's an advantage for small and medium-sized businesses. Ingenuity is central to fast company culture, yet creative reserves are at an all-time low in corporate America. There has never been a more opportune time for heretics, rogues, and heretic rogue marketers to question everything.

In 2006, after a year of traveling and tweaking a business plan, Birds Barbershop scored an SBA loan at a local bank fair. We had a name but no character, so I called Prentice for Door Number 3's help. Today, our brand identity and the way we present ourselves is all them, yet we never inked our character until recently. I took Prentice's advice and worked out a positioning statement in twelve words or less:

"Birds makes salon-quality haircuts affordable and fun. And there's free beer."

That's twelve words exactly if you count the contraction. It's weak though.

"Birds takes the chore out of getting a haircut."

That's closer, but not exactly thrilling. Then I remembered the best press we ever got, a client snippet in an alternative weekly publication:

"Birds' haircuts get you laid."

Sometimes you just have to listen to your customer—

and in my case, the advice of a restaurant manager in a Tasmanian Devil tie and his empowering accomplice, Prentice Howe.

INTRODUCTION

In 2004, my family and I moved to Austin from Los Angeles. We were temporarily staying in my sister's back house, and it was one of those long, dry Texas summers with not much rain. Come October, though, it was thunderstorm after thunderstorm, the rain coming harder seemingly every night. That was also the year the Boston Red Sox were down zero to three in the American League Championship Series, and it felt as if the season was coming to a close much like it had the preceding eighty-six seasons—with a loss.

Something was different that year, though. I could feel it. I could see it through the Texas rain.

The Red Sox hadn't won a World Series since they beat the Cubs in six games in 1918, and there they were, down in the 2004 ALCS, battling the curse of the Bambino, decades of bad endings—oh, and the New York Yankees. You may have heard of the Yankees—the evil empire, the overspenders.

Over the years, it's safe to say Boston had developed into a kind of junior varsity team for New York. Theater shows audition in Boston and open on Broadway in the Big Apple. Boston has cute swan boats, but the Brooklyn Cruise Terminal is where the *Queen Mary* docks. Boston has the Emerald Necklace designed by renowned landscape architect Frederick Law Olmsted, but Olmsted's greatest legacy is New York's Central Park.

So, in 2004 when the entire Red Sox nation held our collective breath as we watched our beloved band of misfits compete against the Yankees, it became bigger than baseball. The Red Sox players—Kevin Millar, Johnny Damon, Pedro Martinez, Curt Schilling, Manny Ramirez, David Ortiz, Kevin Youkilis, and others—were the ultimate challengers. They were notorious for taking shots of whiskey before games, driving motorcycles, growing out their beards, and shaving their heads. They smeared pine tar all over their batting helmets and proudly called themselves "the idiots" (coined by Millar). They were unabashed, free of pretense, and completely authentic.

And they changed history.

The Red Sox came back that year from a three-game deficit to beat the Yankees in four consecutive games before eventually sweeping the St. Louis Cardinals for a World Series Championship.

Sports never make me cry, so it's no surprise I didn't shed a tear when the Red Sox won the World Series that year. I did, however, cry when they came back and beat the Yanks during that wet Texas October. Why? The story of the triumphant 2004 Boston Red Sox transcends baseball and speaks to what it means to be a true empowered challenger. Opening-day payroll for the 2004 Red Sox was $125 million to the Yankees' $182 million—an outspending of $57 million. The Red Sox excelled in the same areas as empowered challenger brands: They didn't outspend, but they were able to outthink and outwork even their toughest competitor.

It's obvious that I love the Red Sox, but that fact alone also represents everything I cherish about my career and my passion: the challenger spirit, the driven mind-set, and the rise of those with relentless ambition. It was all so amazing to me, but do you know what? None of it was an accident.

Former Red Sox CEO Larry Lucchino and the rest of the top brass had made it their life's work to defeat the curse of the Bambino, the dark cloud that had hung over Boston for so many years. It was actually the club's official outward-facing mission statement, written at the beginning of an eight-page team manifesto at the front of the team press guide. It read: "To end the curse of the Bambino and win a World Championship for Boston, New England, and the Red Sox Nation." Talk about a focused positioning for the entire world to see!

In a way, the 2004 Red Sox remind me of David versus Goliath. You see, it's not that David—or the Red Sox—ever wanted you to look at him as the underdog, because that would imply he was unfit to win. That was never the case—far from it. Both were confident competitors who delighted in being underestimated, and that steady confidence coupled with sheer ability led them to win.

David had a sling, after all, not a child's toy. It was a precision instrument that, when used properly, became a devastating weapon equivalent to a .45 caliber handgun. David hit Goliath between the eyes, and he refused to wear armor. Why? Sure, it was shiny, but he was the only one who realized that armor would slow him down.

Those perceived advantages the big companies have

are just like that armor—they can mask even bigger disadvantages.

Just as David had five stones to defeat Goliath, there are five personality traits your brand can leverage to topple your giants. The 2004 Red Sox did just that. They were a team of **lightning rods**, unapologetically themselves in such a way that delighted those who loved them most. They embodied the personality of **compulsive servitude**, serving each other, the organization, and the Red Sox Nation in a way that no team before them had ever done. In the end, it was that act of compulsive servitude—that purposefully authentic personality—that became the very definition of the 2004 Red Sox brand. With Theo Epstein at the helm and new statistical evaluation tools and methods to evaluate players, they were extremely **heretical**—redefining perspectives and changing the game. They were innovative and forward-thinking on and off the field, embodying **constant evolution.** Ownership, for example, continually found new ways to squeeze growth and revenue out of Fenway Park, MLB's oldest stadium. They also questioned orthodoxy by changing business models, putting seats at the top of the Green Monster ballpark, and investing heavily into their local regional cable sports network, NESN. And boy, did they know how to **foster rejection**, happily pushing away the masses in order to embolden their most ardent fans—one of which, if you couldn't tell, is writing this book.

I'm a lot of other things besides a die-hard Red Sox fan, though. I'm a husband, a father of two, and the owner of Door Number 3, an Austin-based brand development and integrated communications firm that champions empowered challenger brands.

So what does that mean, exactly? If you think challengers today are merely the companies chasing "number one" in their industry, you're missing the boat. It's bigger than that. Today's true challengers are brands and companies that are changing the entire game—that means creating better life experiences for consumers through better user experiences. That means making us question our assumptions. That means creating alignment around our passion to change paradigms.

Challenger brands solve the problems often born of the frustrations of our collective desire for a better way of doing things. They delight, they surprise, and they're bursting at the seams with passion.

The difference between a challenger and an empowered challenger isn't the drive—it's the tools and the plan. It's not enough to sit on the sidelines and dream up ways to

“

THOSE PERCEIVED ADVANTAGES THE BIG COMPANIES HAVE ARE JUST LIKE THAT ARMOR—THEY CAN MASK EVEN BIGGER DISADVANTAGES.

”

topple the giants of your industry. **To be truly empowered, you need the road map and the game plan to get there.** You have to know how to uncover, express, and amplify the unique brand personality that makes you tick, and then you have to leverage it for maximum success. Anyone can challenge, but it takes a special company (or a special team like the 2004 Red Sox) to be an empowered challenger.

Whether you're in advertising, marketing, or serving in any capacity as a creative professional faced with the challenges of having to help clients, this book serves as your challenger's playbook to becoming empowered and toppling the giants in your market, even—and perhaps especially—if you're faced with limitations in budget, resources, awareness, or market share.

Hell, maybe you're already a giant. You still might want to take a peek at this discussion of how to continue to outinnovate and outthink. Don't worry—we won't tell anyone.

In the coming chapters, I'll explain the importance of brand positioning and narrowing your audience, and I'll do it using real language with real examples. (Buzzwords, be gone.) I'll also delve into the five brand personality traits of an empowered challenger and the advantages of each, and you'll learn how your brand can use them to find success.

Let's play ball, shall we?

EMBRACE YOUR CHALLENGER-ABILITY

The role of the challenger transcends the business world: Remember *The Little Engine That Could*, the classic children's tale by Watty Piper? And who wasn't rooting for Rudy in the 1993 inspirational football flick that was about so much more than the sport? From Davy Crockett to Rocky, Erin Brockovich to Jackie Robinson, challengers have come in all shapes and sizes. All of them had the decks stacked against them and were obvious challengers, but many are hiding in plain sight.

Take, for example, linen—such a great fabric, flattering and comfortable, yet not allowed to come out of the closet after Labor Day. Who made that rule? Who knows, but it's a reality poor linen will always face. There are plenty more products destined to challenge. Now that we've got liquid soaps in fancy packaging and any scent you can dream up, poor bar soap has been shelved (often literally). If you were the parents of a toddler, why would you choose shoelaces over the convenience of Velcro? Then there are black jelly beans, always the last left in the package. Oh, and it's practically a universal truth that broccoli gets better recipes than cauliflower.

In all seriousness, embracing your challenger-ability is all about understanding that boundless ambition and the ability to outthink are what it takes to topple the giants that overshadow us. This is the reality of a challenger, whether we're talking about a product, a character, or a vegetable. Even J. K. Rowling was rejected twelve times before a publisher accepted *Harry Potter and The Philosopher's Stone*. Even then, it was only because the chairman of the publisher, Bloomsbury, had a child who just would not drop it. (See, I'm talking about leveraging pint-sized resources, people.)

Before you break out the tissues and violins for the ghosts of challengers past, present, and future, though, know that being a challenger is an opportunity, not a burden. I know the word *challenger* itself can sound discouraging, but it's actually a really exciting place to be. This is especially true in today's economy when so many challengers are actually the change-makers, redefining not only the rules but also the game. If you're ambitious and have the right toolbox, you can overcome.

This is true even if the need to overcome isn't immediate. Even if you're an enterprise giant, rarely—and by rarely, I mean never—are you eating bonbons on your Italian leather sectional and counting your cash, smiling as you stare down the barrel of twenty years of positive projections. There's always a reason to maintain that challenger spirit, to look over your shoulder and assess the trajectory of companies that are embracing their challenger-abilities.

Maybe the sofa is a hand-me-down made of pleather, your chocolate stash consists of your kids' unwanted Halloween candy, and your projections are less than stellar—it doesn't matter. All your perceived disadvantages can actually be the things that allow you to move quickly and make decisions while dodging a gauntlet of stakeholders and layers. If you know what you're doing, you can make strategic moves to your advantage.

It comes down to this: regardless of the size of your business, you have to stay ahead of maintaining your position, your voice, and your tight brand positioning while tapping into the five "empowered challenger" personality traits to be successful.

LEVERAGING LIMITATIONS TO WIN

Brands today are facing a new reality. The playing field has changed, and you're expected to do more with less. I've seen this narrative in the more than twenty years I've been working in advertising. New or returning clients continue to come to us here at Door Number 3 with budgets that are stretched or categories flooded by new contenders, yet expectations are always higher year after year.

It's reminiscent of the television show *MacGyver*. Here's your bobby pin, toothpick, and rubber band. Diffuse the bomb. Figure it out.

Once we prove we can do just that, we develop an appetite to do *even more* with *even less*. As Sir Ernest Rutherford said, "We have no money, so we will have to outthink." Successfully outthinking is a drug for brands that have figured out that resourcefulness is a form of creativity. Being resourceful forces you to change your perspective and shake things up. Oftentimes, playing in a smaller sandbox is one form of leveraging your limitations, as knowing where your boundaries are can actually liberate you to solve problems in entirely new ways.

There's another aspect to this new reality: brands aren't in control—consumers are. In the *Mad Men* era, traditional media was an easy way to reach a captive audience. You could dream up a fun campaign, put it on one of the major networks, and people would see it. Why? There was no fast-forwarding commercials, no ad blocking, no smartphones for distraction. Back then, brands were put on a pedestal—entitled, if you will, by the essentially guaranteed consumption of whatever they were spewing.

Things couldn't be more opposite today. We're all distracted, and often we're looking at two devices at once—sometimes three. Choices for devices and platforms abound, so the power really is in the hands of those who are sharing the story—that is, consumers.

In this digital age, your brand is discovered more effectively when a customer passes it on to friends and family. Word-of-mouth marketing is all about spreading the love for your brand organically and with authenticity, but this phenomenon doesn't just magically happen. **You have to give people the tools and the resources to be able to effectively share your story, and the best way to do that is to make it become part of theirs.**

What does that mean, exactly? All those interesting Twitter posts, memorable videos, and bits of engaging content build your brand's personality. Customers will want to pass on that personality through sharing because they're empowered to be a part of your brand experience more than ever. Yes, some of the sharing is out of your control, so you'll need to be willing to let go to a degree. To achieve long-term success, though, you must do all you can to influence what they pass on by arming them with what they'll need to ultimately help you do your job. That starts with clearing a pathway that leads to advocacy, and there are four steps in that process: differentiation, fascination, consistency, and ultimately advocacy.

DIFFERENTIATION

Differentiation is critical—not just because it's the first step in your journey to create a pathway to brand advocacy, but also because it forces you to identify a blindingly clear proposition. What makes your brand special in a way no other brand can claim?

An example of a brand nailing differentiation is SodaStream, whose tagline is "water made exciting." By creating home carbonation machines for the masses, they went after an industry ruled by giants in a refreshing way. SodaStream's story is rooted in social and environmental responsibility. Americans alone dispose of 130 billion bottles and cans every year, but with their product, you can use your own tap water and return the gas cylinders. As part of their global ad push, they released a commercial in 2012 called "The SodaStream Effect" that depicted thousands of bottles and cans that spontaneously vanish when someone uses their SodaStream soda maker at home. The voice-over says, "With SodaStream, you can save two thousand bottles a year. If you love bubbles, set them free."

That's differentiation. They could have mentioned that their bubbles are fizzier than the competition's, that their machines are more convenient than driving to the convenience store for a soda fix, or that their products can save soda drinkers hundreds of dollars a year. But they didn't. SodaStream aligned with a higher calling, taking on a billion-dollar industry and decades of indifference about waste and recycling. While they're no mom-and-pop business, they're certainly an example of a challenger that not only differentiated beautifully but also understood the magnetic power of doing so unabashedly.

In 2011, Kristen Harp, SodaStream's US marketing manager, said, "Then and now we've had very little budget for traditional media spend. We've built this business, an entire category in fact, on the back of word-of-mouth and PR." It's paid off.

FASCINATION

Fascination is the second step to clearing that pathway to advocacy, and it's all about uncovering your inner remarkability. That means using every opportunity, every touch point, and every moment to your advantage. Especially when you don't have the ability to outspend, you can't waste any surface—even down to the bottom or inside panel of your packaging.

A brand that has succeeded in finding and embracing their inner remarkability is the Mini Cooper. It launched into an industry that's a veritable stomping ground for giants, and it was a small vehicle coming out during the season of McMansions and gas-guzzling SUVs. Mini Cooper didn't have the ability to outspend their competition, so they had to outthink them.

How did they do it? They orchestrated stunts. They created amazing outdoor boards that interacted with the environment in ways nobody had ever dreamed to do. I remember a two-page magazine spread in particular in which Mini Cooper had the publication change the color of the staples from ordinary gray to bright orange. Nothing major, right? It wouldn't be ordinarily, but Mini Cooper's spread was mostly white space. The way the art was directed made the final piece look like an overhead shot of a Mini Cooper weaving between the staples, with those little orange staples serving as street cones. Everything about that print ad and that brand was centered on celebrating small at a time when the United States was all about big. They never wasted an opportunity to be fascinating.

CONSISTENCY

Consistency is the third step, and it's an important one. Consistency starts with enforcing restraint so your core story can shine even brighter. This sounds simple enough, but it's not. One of the hardest things for our clients has traditionally been resisting the temptation to say everything, to be all things to all people. I've seen "something for everyone" in creative briefs throughout the years at different agencies more times than I can count. Marketers see it as a selling point, but I've always known it as the kiss of death.

Think of it this way. Imagine I'm holding three tennis balls. If I toss all three of them at you at once, you might catch one, *maybe* two. If I toss one at you, though, you're guaranteed to catch it every time. It's the same with your brand's messaging. You get moments, milliseconds even, to engage or share your story. If you overburden with too many tennis balls, you're confusing your audience and sabotaging your ad spend.

Take, for example, the menu at the Cheesecake Factory. It was a one-pager in 1978, and it is now twenty-one pages. It's so gigantic that it drops to the table with a giant thud. In true "something for everyone" style, you can get an Asian noodle dish, lasagna, hot wings—oh, yeah, and cheesecake. And you can order any one of more than 250 other dishes they serve daily. Stack that up against a popular burger stand we have here in Austin called P.Terry's. The menu is simple, the ingredients are fresh, and their commitment to serving quality, all-natural ingredients that you can pronounce is admirable. Sure, they could probably add cobb salads or spring rolls to the menu board, but that just doesn't make sense. P.Terry's is focused.

In addition to keeping the product and the message simple, consistency also means having constancy of purpose and not veering off script to chase shiny objects. This is hard for brands because internal teams get tired of their messaging long before the consumer does. It makes sense, after all. They're tweaking it constantly. It's on their desktop, their emails, their trade-show booth, even the background on their smartphones. Sometimes, it's hard to remember that the audience doesn't see it as much. It takes guts to stick with a message or a campaign for a while after a brand births it into the consumers' world.

I'm not advocating staying in one lane for decades and

not shifting messaging when the time is right, but there is power in consistency, especially when it comes to a smart usage of marketing dollars. When you don't have a lot of them, having restraint and staying the course can be key. Remaining true to your brightest differentiators and steadfast in your mission to keep the brand fascinating isn't always easy, but it's the only way to ultimately achieve the advocacy of your consumer.

ADVOCACY

Advocacy is the final step, the culmination of a journey through the first three stops along a now-cleared path. You can turn customers into advocates by giving them not only your story but also the ability to *communicate with* and even *participate in* what makes your brand special. People won't line up at your door because they want to passively witness or listen; they'll line up at your door because they want to contribute and give feedback.

An example of advocacy in action came from none other than my wife. One afternoon, we were inching along a chronically congested highway in Austin. There was an accident off to the side of the road. Then, this happened:

Wife, riding shotgun, reaching for her phone: "Hold on, I've got to do something."

Me: "What are you doing?"

Wife: "I've got to tell my fellow Wazers about this one."

Me: "What? On your Waze app?"

Wife: "Yeah. I'm just going to report that there's an accident off to the shoulder. I get points."

Me, intrigued: "Oh, points? What are the points for? Do we get a free Crock-Pot if you rack up enough?"

Wife: "I have no idea what they're for, but it's cool. I just know I get points."

This little story makes me chuckle, but it also makes me appreciate even more the true value of advocacy. It doesn't take much, and it doesn't even have to be monetary. The path to advocacy is all about opening the lines of communication so your audience feels as if they're a part of the brand.

Clearing a pathway to advocacy is just one way your brand can look to leveraging limitations as a way to win through challenger-ability. That's only the sunny side, though. The truth is that everyone faces obstacles as they seek to become empowered challengers. Maybe it's a lack of resources in your marketing department, or maybe you're dealing with a company culture that's going to have a hard time embracing positioning and redefining your brand's story. Even your industry giants have obstacles—maybe they're often sidelined by the inability to move quickly or are weighed down by the gauntlet of decision makers.

The reality is that both big and small brands all face big and small obstacles. The key to overcoming them is to view them not as disadvantages but as opportunities. So, if you can't outspend, you must outthink. How?

You start with brand positioning.

BRAND POSITIONING: WHAT IT IS, WHAT IT ISN'T, WHY IT MATTERS

Brand positioning is a way your brand can begin the process of outthinking your competition. It brings clarity to your internal communications, marketing strategies, advertising campaigns, and promotional tactics. **It's so vital, in fact, that a clear brand positioning statement is the cornerstone to being able to challenge in the first place.**

That's important. Seriously, read it again. Becoming an empowered challenger *has* to start here, at the difficult and uncomfortable spot where your brand positioning gets real.

This exercise is hard, and that's why many companies don't do it. Most people don't like to stand naked in front of the mirror and ask, "What do we have here?" They don't want to sit across the room from all their stakeholders or investors or team members and challenge the status quo, continuously asking why. Instead, they just keep coasting because they can—you know, things are working okay, and they're doing just fine.

It's easier *not* to do this. You've got to be willing to stare down your positioning statement until you get to that core, distilled set of words that's going to inform everything you do moving forward—business decisions, creative decisions, marketing decisions, messaging decisions—all the way down to how you answer the phone.

Not ready? Put down the book, and pick it back up again when you are.

Still with me? Good.

What you must remember about a brand positioning statement is this: **It doesn't just say *what* you are—it says *why* you are.** It's a mix of rational and emotional.

“

YOU'VE GOT TO BE WILLING TO STARE DOWN YOUR POSITIONING STATEMENT UNTIL YOU GET TO THAT CORE, DISTILLED SET OF WORDS THAT'S GOING TO INFORM EVERYTHING YOU DO MOVING FORWARD.

”

It's differentiating. It's concise, believable, memorable, and motivating. It informs your business goals as well as every piece of communication moving forward, internally and externally—and that's just the starting point.

In short, well-defined brand positioning isn't a luxury—it's table stakes. Interestingly enough, I've found birthing a new brand positioning statement is also one of the most misunderstood processes out there.

Why? Almost all my clients ask something like, "What am I going to get out of this? We don't get a new campaign? We don't get a new color palette? Is it seriously just words on a page?"

The answer is always a wholehearted yes. It's just words on a page.

At the outset, that doesn't sound very appealing to business owners, founders, CEOs, and check writers. As we work through the process, though, it becomes illuminating. In fact, the brand positioning process is the most illuminating part of everything we go through with our clients at Door Number 3. And, at the end, it puts all those skeptical stakeholders in lockstep.

What we deliver is a positioning platform with reasons to

believe, an elevator statement, and brand truths incorporated into a manifesto. It's proudly taped on cubicle walls and beside computer monitors in the C-suite as a reminder that everyone is to be speaking the same language. **In a sense, the brand positioning process is like therapy for brands.** They're lying on the hypothetical couch, really thinking about business goals, reprioritizing communication points, and asking themselves why their brand exists in the first place. What they discover will carve the path for creating campaigns that work, campaigns that propel challengers.

Now, quickly: tell me your brand's positioning statement in twelve words or less. Remember, it's not a tagline. It's an internal, high-level statement that clearly articulates the benefits that will most resonate with and create action with your target audiences. The most powerful positioning statements contain both rational and emotional levers, becoming the strategic spark for your entire brand ethos.

WHAT MAKES A POOR POSITIONING STATEMENT?

Not having a positioning statement is bad, but not nearly as bad as having an ineffective one you deem to be good. How can you tell stellar positioning statements from the mere fillers? Look for one of the following warning signs:

- **It's puffery.** I was recently in line at the airport behind a business traveler who had his company's elevator statement emblazoned across his luggage tag. He worked for an upstart energy company in the Midwest. The copy was about one hundred words long with over twenty adjectives and ten commas. It read more like the ingredients list on a Cheetos bag than anything related to a brand. If your positioning inspires marketing messages that are laden with superlatives and run-on sentences, it's time to bust out the red pen. It all goes back to consistency, really. After all, consistency's partner is often simplicity. Don't create something that's so overwritten that it tries to say everything and ends up saying nothing.

- **It's noncommittal.** I heard a story about a mechanic who created a marquee reading, "Proudly serving imports and domestics." In case you missed it, that's *every* car. Later, he wasn't getting much business, so he changed it to specifically serving one brand of automobiles: Volkswagen. Guess what? His business started to flourish. VW owners from miles away specifically sought him out. This just shows that although closing little doors can be hard for brands, oftentimes one big one will open as a result. Here's some perspective: David Baker, a Nashville-based strategic consultant, has made the case that brands without clear positioning are simply driving around in a white van with a serious stack of interchangeable door magnets. Their service—and their magnet—changes all too often. Pet sitting? Lawn-care services? Roofing? This "take your pick" brand mentality is a recipe for disaster. Sooner or later, you're going to have to recycle your magnets, commit to something, and *paint the van.* Look at the brands we all love like REI, Nike, Whole Foods, and Apple—their positioning is anything but wishy-washy. Rather, they're specific. They've painted the van, and that's the way to grow.

- **It's inward-facing.** Ever gone on a first date and talked incessantly about yourself the whole time, never inquiring about the person sitting quietly across the table (you know, the one who keeps inconspicuously glancing at her watch)? I'm going to bet that didn't end well. It's the same for your brand. Stop using phrases like "industry leading," "innovating," and "fastest growing." Many clients come to us with what they think is a positioning statement. Then they explain it, and it's all inside baseball. Certain industries are particularly guilty of this. (I'm talking to you, tech companies.) They throw in buzzwords that don't mean a hell of a lot to their audience but sure make their corporate executives feel good. Watch season one of HBO's *Silicon Valley*, and you'll see what I mean. If we assume that the job of a brand positioning is to uniquely connect to the customer in a way that is wholly distinct from your competition, then meaningless chest thumping is a waste of time. Leave it out.

POSITIONING STATEMENTS DONE RIGHT

Empowered challengers have a crisp, clear positioning statement. Take Southwest Airlines, for example. Since adopting its current name in 1971, they've democratized the skies by empowering their people to let their personalities and individuality shine. And where did it all start? It came from their culture, from their ethos built around freedom. Brand positioning should start at this authentic place, built on the truth of who you are and then championed from the inside out because of your people.

Another example is apparel company Criquet Shirts. Imagine the preppiness of New England mixed with the laid-back Austin vibe. Do you have that in your head? Now, note that they call their throwback, vintage shirts "player's shirts" and market them as being "for the nineteenth hole." This positioning is spot-on, as it puts you in that relaxing headspace of wherever *your* nineteenth hole is. It's probably with friends, and it's the best part of the day. Now you can see why the brand is more than just another golf shirt—it's a lifestyle. It's also differentiating—after all, the world needed another polo shirt like it needed a hole in the head. Criquet has tailored an incredibly unique positioning, and it fits.

EMBOLDENED BY A POWER OF BELIEF

Author and speaker Simon Sinek is famous for popularizing the concept of "start with why." In his words, "people don't care what you do—they care why you do it." That's struck a chord with marketers and everyone involved with branding, and there's good reason for that. Do you know why you get out of bed in the morning, why you do what you do? Once you wrap your arms around that big aha, it informs so much. It informs how you're going to overcome obstacles. It informs your next growth strategy. It informs how you nurture company culture and how you approach the market for your product.

It's called belief. Belief is the first step to bringing out your challenger within. It's why you do what you do. It determines your business goals and helps you avoid obstacles. Belief exudes a persona that evolves customers into advocates. When they believe what you believe, you can't be defeated.

If one of my clients at Door Number 3 lacks the power of belief and is unable to articulate their *why*, we typically hit pause. We slow everything down. We figure that out before we move forward. If you don't believe in yourself and you don't know what your *why* is, how's anyone else going to believe it?

I test my positioning statements by writing a consumer-facing manifesto next—something that might be written on a to-go bag, the About page of a website, or even the side of a shoebox. It's important to note that the manifesto is different from the positioning statement. When I'm working with clients and we're going through the positioning process, we'll get to a statement we believe in. We're nodding our heads. We've got it. That's the flat-footed positioning statement, the filter through which all communication must go. It's the checks and balances. The manifesto, then, is the outward-facing prose inspired by your positioning statement.

If you were a restaurant, what fun headline would you get screen-printed on your T-shirts? What message would you paint on the walls? There are all kinds of places for a manifesto, and the shining examples are those that become inspired messages that are not identical to the brand positioning, but *because of it*.

Chipotle is a prime example of a business that has mastered when, where, and how to share its manifesto that is obviously grounded with strong positioning. Recent food safety snafus aside, they've done an excellent example of integrating their "food integrity" everywhere you look, from their drink cups to their website.

The moral of the story is this: pair a strong belief with a strong positioning, and you'll be unstoppable. **Only when your positioning statement is ready can your brand truly become an empowered challenger.** After all, you can't make a sword when it's not hot enough to be malleable. Is your steel hot enough to bend, to evolve, to be redefined? You can fortify the future of your brand by fortifying your positioning statement now.

FIVE PERSONALITY TRAITS OF EMPOWERED CHALLENGERS

Just like David had five stones to defeat Goliath, you have five personality traits of empowered challengers that are accessible to you at any time. Grab one. Grab more. Grab whatever makes sense for you to defeat your giants.

- **Lightning Rod:** Where do photographers point their lenses when the sky begins to darken and the thunder starts crackling? Lightning rods. Lady Gaga is a lightning rod. It wasn't just about her wearing a dress made of meat; it was about her doing the unexpected. Love her or hate her, you'll never forget her. Outside of the music space, lightning-rod brands are unabashed and truthful. They exude a charismatic attraction. What Lady Gaga is to music, Elon Musk is to electricity.

- **Heretical:** Also called redefining perspective, heretical brands change the game, not just the rules. They look over the horizon and discover what people will need in the future, and they bring it to them ahead of schedule. Amazon and Virgin are examples of heretical brands.

- **Fostering Rejection:** Fostering rejection is all about resisting the desire to be all things to all people in order to attract your most ardent fans. These brands happily build smaller core groups of fans by pushing away the masses, and those core fans become their biggest advocates. As a result, they see exponential growth. CrossFit is an example of a brand that's had great success from fostering rejection.

- **Compulsive Servitude:** Compulsive servitude means overdelivering to the extent that it becomes the very definition of your brand. This isn't just smiling or telling customers to have a good day—it's finding unique ways to serve that are true to your brand identity and that create completely memorable experiences. The Ritz-Carlton learns the smallest desires of its guests so they can be granted without request. That's compulsive servitude.

- **Constant Evolution:** Brands that have mastered constant evolution remain category neutral. They're inventors at heart, looking for ways to demonstrate their core values in new product categories after establishing trust in another. This personality trait has led Apple to create watches and Shinola to make turntables.

METHOD'S METHOD TO POSITIONING ITSELF AS A CHALLENGER

One brand winning with strong positioning and an even stronger adherence to one of the five personality traits is method, one of my favorite brands. Whoever thought a hand-soap bottle that you put on your sink could be beautiful or that the execution of their brand story could be just as beautiful? Well, that's exactly what they've done. The company was started by two guys who wanted to make cleaning products they didn't have to hide under the sink, creating them without "dirty" ingredients. Their call to arms is appropriately "people against dirty," and they've focused their entire company around speed and innovation. While industry giants might take years to bring a new product to market, method can do the same in a matter of weeks.

In every way possible—through their entire design, aesthetic, approach to research and development, and brand ethos—method is a heretical company. Speaking to that last point, method has what they call a "human-festo" on their website—talk about a power of belief—that includes delightful statements such as, "While we love a freshly detoxed home, we think perfect is boring and weirdly-ness is next to godliness." Consumers can get behind that bold personality, and the brand continues to rally people around their quest to "fear no mess."

So, how does a brand come to embody a personality trait like method embodies heretical? You have to start by going through an empowered challenger exercise. Take a hard look at each of the five personality traits, and find ways—actionable ways—that you could identify with them.

Here's an example. Say you're a restaurant that's gone through brand positioning and has determined you're a farm-to-table concept committed to reducing your carbon footprint by serving only locally sourced ingredients. You don't ship in your produce from Central America; you gather it from local sources for maximum freshness. In a world of chain restaurants serving processed, prepackaged foods, that's what differentiates you; it's what makes you special. Now ask yourself: How can we be a lightning-rod personality around that?

Let's spitball.

For example, what if you created a "cantaloupe cam" to track the journey of fruit to your competitors' dining room versus yours. By strapping a GoPro to those fruit crates, you'd be able to show two different paths: one of a cantaloupe coming from a faraway land and ending up at your rival, and one of a cantaloupe grown at a family farm down the road that *you* serve mere hours later. You'd have built a lightning-rod way to tell your story—after all, who could ignore the cantaloupe cam exposé dedicated to making your point?

This whole exercise is about running through the personality traits and seeing what clicks with your brand positioning. In that spirit, consider another scenario with another fictitious restaurant, only this time you're aiming to embody the trait of compulsive servitude. You're going to overdeliver such that it becomes the very definition of the brand. Through brand positioning, you've determined that what makes your restaurant unique is that your servers have culinary knowledge like no other restaurant in proximity. Chain diners haven't got anything on your servers, so you decide to call your staffers "culinerds"—culinary nerds. It's catchy, but it's not a joke. You coin the term, and you live it. Do your foodie guests want to know more about the IPA on tap and what exactly makes it so hoppy? Do they want to understand the subtle differences between king and sockeye salmon? Talk to your culinerds.

The two scenarios above are merely examples to get your wheels turning. To discover how your brand can embody a personality trait that fits, try going through an exercise to generate ideas that are both ownable and able to set you apart. To start, grab a pad of sticky notes, set a timer for fifteen minutes, and begin writing down one idea per sheet. Don't overthink. Don't edit. Don't stop. Just keep writing until the buzzer sounds. Then, post them on the wall. Move them around, elevating the ideas that stand out and ignoring the rest. You're bound to come away with at least a few gems worth pursuing.

☆ CHALLENGE YOURSELF ☆

WHAT'S YOUR BRAND POSITIONING STATEMENT?

Remember, we're talking about the North Star statement through which all communications will be filtered as you move forward. To get there, start by thinking about what your company offers your target audience that others in your category don't.

Here's an example to get you started. I've never seen Southwest's positioning statement (remember, these aren't typically consumer-facing statements), but I imagine it to have punchy thoughts like "short-haul," "no frills" and "low-priced." It's likely the kind of no-BS, anti-status-quo copy that would inspire the wonderful consumer-facing tagline, "You are now free to move about the country." Remember that one? And "Ding!"—that memorable mnemonic device that accompanied it? That's exactly what a brand positioning statement is born to do—inspire storytelling that hits consumers on a visceral level.

So, ask yourself: "What does our target market want and need that only we can deliver?" Crafting the actual positioning statement requires some trial and error, but the framework is usually something like this:

For (target audience who ______), (your brand) is the only one that delivers (point of differentiation) because only (your brand) is (reason to believe).

Once you have something in place, go on a fluff-finding mission. Grab a red pen and trim liberally until only the essential words remain. Then ask yourself: "Is it believable? Does it resonate with our target? Is it uniquely ownable? Does it inspire me and my team to get out of bed each morning?" If you've answered yes to all four questions, you're not just on your way to a brilliant brand story. You're on your way to stealing market share and toppling giants.

EMPOWERED CHALLENGER TAKEAWAYS

As we conclude this chapter, you must remember these three points:

1. Learn to leverage your limitations to win through your challenger-ability, starting with creating a clear pathway to advocacy.

2. Having a poor brand positioning statement you think is phenomenal is worse than having none at all. You must start with brand

positioning to move forward as an empowered challenger. This is not optional.

3. The five personality traits we will discuss in this book are: lightning rod, heretical, fostering rejection, compulsive servitude, and constant evolution. You can leverage one or several, as long as your choice(s) helps propel your brand forward.

TURN CUSTOMERS INTO ADVOCATES

Without the advocacy of your customer, you can never successfully challenge. You can't gain the advocacy of your customers, though, if you don't really know them.

I have a good entrepreneur friend I have nicknamed One Data Point Barry. He gets input from one source (sometimes himself) before charging forward with the full belief he has the answer. His data point, in his opinion, is bulletproof.

Really, his one data point is just a lone reference in what should be a much larger assessment.

With One Data Point Barry, we have lively conversations in which he'll wax poetic on certain topics he has spent no time researching. It's somewhat on the hilarious side, but it speaks to something larger: your brand has to question assumptions and go beyond them, sourcing multiple data points to determine if you're even pursuing the right audience.

We talk to our clients about this very subject all the time. Are you funneling the right amount of time, money, and resources into the right audience investments? What if you work diligently to get your message dialed in, only to later realize you've been talking to the wrong group the entire time?

In short, knowing your audience well isn't just something you *ought* to do. It's something you *have* to do. It's the price of entry. To do it well, you'll need to do your homework and leverage that data against the competition.

To start, never let anyone on your team try to convince you that your audience is everyone. Instead, segment and prioritize your customers. Examine geographic and demographic information. Don't just seek data—stockpile it. Make first-party data a priority. Capture audience insights using online tools such as Google Analytics. Conduct phone interviews, focus groups, email surveys, and customer intercepts.

Throughout it all, though, look for insights beyond age, gender, and geography. Those do matter, but try and answer big-picture questions. What motivates an audience's purchasing decisions? How long does it take to push a customer down the purchase funnel? What kind of comparative shopping is common within this group? What touch points along the customer journey are the most impactful from their perspective?

Once you've graphed the motivations that are influencing customers, you can adapt your marketing plan to ensure they're highly engaged. Taking this sponge perspective puts you in a prime place to take action based on your research—and taking action, after all, is what the fastest-growing brands are doing today.

These rising companies are able to leverage audience insights to do much more than just influence behavior. They're actually influencing culture, changing the vernacular, and turning predictability inside out. How? By putting marketing at the center of it all—operations, R&D, HR. Smart companies know marketing isn't an isolated discipline, off to the side that's only there to increase sales. Rather, it's the one team that has a beat on what's happening elsewhere within the business. It's the core.

That's what these brands *are* doing today, but what they

aren't doing is blindly dumping money into one-way communication channels. Instead, by truly knowing their customers, they've mastered the art of advocacy and harnessed the power of word-of-mouth.

Advocacy is vital because your brand no longer controls the message—customers do. Customers control what, when, and where they get all their information. **You can't buy your way into being interesting and getting noticed like you used to, and it's changed everything for marketers.** As a business today, you have to be willing to give up control. What you lose there, though, you can make up for by bolstering the power of your brand message. Make it so strong that there's no mistaking its meaning when it gets into the hands of your customers, your potential advocates. You're going to help them understand what you represent and what you stand for. When they start sharing your content, videos, blog posts, and more, they've become your messengers.

That doesn't just *happen*, though. People share what makes them look interesting, relevant, and smart. That's not just my opinion—it's science. There's an entire psychology behind why we're wired to share, and studies on the nucleus accumbens link strong connections between social platforms and the brain's reward system. How can you capitalize? Putting the power of share into the hands

"

ADVOCACY IS VITAL BECAUSE YOUR BRAND NO LONGER CONTROLS THE MESSAGE—CUSTOMERS DO. CUSTOMERS CONTROL WHAT, WHEN, AND WHERE THEY GET ALL THEIR INFORMATION.

"

of your advocates is the answer, and equipping them with the tools and the stories they need is the first step.

Apparel company REI is an example of a brand that has mastered the art of fostering advocacy, and their #OptOutside campaign is a true representation of that. This is a company that wears its bigger purpose on its sleeve—its flannel shirtsleeve, that is—by believing life outdoors is a life well lived. It's fitting, then, that they turned Black Friday on its head by encouraging everyone—even their very own customers and employees—to #OptOutside instead of visiting brick-and-mortar stores. They were so dedicated that they closed all their 145 stores on the biggest shopping day of the year, giving all their twelve thousand employees a day to enjoy the outdoors. As a brand, REI has a higher calling and a strong power of belief, and this campaign became a platform to express that.

And it worked.

REI's #OptOutside campaign won numerous advertising awards, but it did much more than that. The lifelong bond created between the brand and its consumers through value alignment easily trumped whatever was lost in post-Thanksgiving revenue.

#OptOutside wasn't REI's first push to winning the advocacy of their audience—in fact, far from it. They've consistently relied on dedicated customers submitting breathtaking photos of themselves using actual REI gear, providing modern-day, real-time testimonials and a steady stream of user-generated content. It's brilliant. It's ongoing. It's a great example of a brand mastering social currency and the art of advocacy.

Warby Parker is another visionary brand to emulate when you're trying to turn customers into advocates. Born out of frustration in 2010, the brand was founded by four students at the Wharton School of the University of Pennsylvania who were sickened by the thought of shelling out $700 to replace a pair of lost glasses. They did their research and saw an opportunity to steal market share from eyewear behemoth Luxottica by moving the shopping experience online. Their new model allows customers to skip the bland strip-mall chain store and instead get stylish—and at long last, *affordable*—eyeglasses and sunglasses by mail, disrupting the entire eyewear industry in the process.

Why did it work? If someone walks up and compliments your glasses, it's unlikely that you're going to respond with a simple "thank you." You're going to share the experience of shopping Warby Parker, mention their unique online platform, and possibly convert someone else into a Warby Parker fan along the way—that's social currency.

FOUR CHARACTERISTICS OF CUSTOMERS MAGNETICALLY ATTRACTED TO CHALLENGER BRANDS

To turn consumers into advocates and win with social currency as successfully as brands like REI and Warby Parker, challenger brands need to attract the *right* customers. The following are four key characteristics of customers that are magnetically attracted to challenger brands (and are most likely to align with the empowered challenger personalities).

THEY WANT TO SHARE THEIR PASSION

The customers of challenger brands want to share the brand's passion. A key example of harnessing the power of a passion is Whole Foods' Declaration of Interdependence. In it, they name their motto, "Whole Foods, Whole People, Whole Planet." This isn't just an empty phrase, though—it's one that's executed. Whole Foods' collective consumer base shops there—even pays high dollars for groceries there—because they share those same values. If I step inside the door of my neighborhood Whole Foods, I'm greeted with a basket of fresh fruit and a sign that reads "Free healthy snacks for kids." Before I can even put my hands on my cart, they've added value to my experience (especially the experience of shopping with two hungry little girls). The fruit basket isn't a huge or expensive gesture, but it gives customers a reason to continue shopping there, and they're likely to share their experience with others. It's a brilliant execution of Whole Foods' Declaration of Interdependence, their power of belief, and their commitment to value alignment—bringing out the passion of the shopper by showcasing the passion of the store.

Then we have Dove, another example of a brand that rallies behind its higher calling. Dove's mission is about something far more profound than just selling soap. Dove leverages its brand to help improve the self-esteem of girls around the globe. Through their #SpeakBeautiful movement, Dove is helping girls gain confidence in their beauty. It's a meaningful message that encourages their loyalists to be part of a shared passion.

THEY WANT TO CONVERT OTHERS

The customers of challenger brands want to convert others to the brand. Consumers' personal brands and their social credibility are inherently linked to the brands they love—and, let's face it, one of those well-loved brands is Target. How many times have you witnessed someone receiving a compliment on an article of clothing? A lot, right? Now, how many times have you heard the person respond with a simple "thanks"? If the clothing was from Target, however, the person probably said a whole lot more. "I got it on sale at Target" is a popular one—or, better yet, he or she might refer to it as "Targét." I've noticed this type of response in particular with my wife and sisters. Would those responses be the same if that blouse were from K-Mart? Walmart? Kohl's? Chico's? Absolutely not. Target has created an affordable but stylish persona, and converting others is a big part of their marketing strategy. The brand encourages advocates to share their experiences with their networks, converting others and growing the tribe.

Social media plays a big part in Target's winning approach. For starters, they don't have a social catchall, but instead they treat each platform with respect. There's a different handle for each customer need on Twitter, for example—from @targetstyle to @targetdeals to @targetnews. They also have strong community management: Target responds to 64 percent of social comments within the hour and 99 percent within twenty-four hours. In addition, the brand isn't afraid to cross-pollinate their different social platforms. Whether it's posting a YouTube video about party-planning tips gleaned from Pinteresters or letting a designer take over their Instagram feed while promoting the event on Facebook, this passion for engaging their customer base through technology helps Target convert clickers into advocates.

THEY WANT TO BE REWARDED

The customers of challenger brands want to be rewarded. Creating brand loyalty should be a challenger brand's end game. How do you get there, though? The majority of customers want to have meaningful relationships with brands, and reward programs can help forge paths in that direction. Here are four simple ways your brand can reward your audience:

1. **Loyalty programs:** Loyalty programs are a wildly popular way to reward because they're accessible and effective. Starbucks is an example of a behemoth brand that maintains an empowered challenger spirit. They've done an excellent job of rewarding customers, linking mobile and in-store experiences with a loyalty program that people love. It can be accessed via a Starbucks card or a mobile app, and people collect stars to be redeemed for free food and drinks. It's gamified, in a sense, as active users also get email offers, early access to new products, and more. Like Starbucks's approach, I've found the best loyalty programs are gamified.

2. **Referral programs:** Lyft—the San Francisco-based ride-sharing company—is an example of a company with a strong referral

program. All riders are given a Lyft code that they can then share with their friends. When someone creates a Lyft account using that code, the person referring is rewarded with a twenty-dollar credit, and the new customer is welcomed with a free ride. It's a simple program that builds credibility and results in a win-win for both the giver and the receiver.

3. **Birthday gifts:** Makeup chain Sephora is masterful when it comes to celebrating a customer's birthday. With their Very Important Beauty Insider (VIB) program, members can choose from a variety of birthday packages that typically include travel-sized products. This brings customers into the store during a special time and—from a sales perspective—opens the possibility that they might leave with more than just their free birthday gift.

4. **Purpose-driven discounts:** Michael Portman, the fellow who wrote the foreword for this book, co-owns Birds Barbershop in Austin. Besides being a truly badass rock-and-roll barbershop, it's also a business that's promoting a healthy lifestyle by offering a fixed discount to anyone who arrives by bike. That's a big deal in Austin—we have too many people, too many cars, and not enough roadways. It's the kind of reward that deepens the bond between the patron and the brand.

Note here that rewarding customers doesn't have to be incredibly expensive for brands. In fact, it doesn't even have to be monetary. Remember that story with my wife and her Waze points? The points themselves aren't so relevant, really. What she loves most is receiving feedback and appreciation from her fellow Wazers. It just goes to show you that doing more with less can redefine your relationship with your customers. It all comes down to how you reward their loyalty.

THEY WANT TO CHANGE PARADIGMS

The consumers most likely to respond to the challenger brand personalities want to change paradigms; they are frustrated by the status quo and see themselves as agents of change (often just like challenger brands themselves). They're the ones asking, "Why do we have to do it the old way? Why can't we reinvent things? Why can't I rent a car that doesn't smell? Why can't someone make a grocery-cart wheel that doesn't wobble? Why are school lunches so bad?"

A brand that has really spoken to the collective desire to change paradigms is Rent Like a Champion, similar to Airbnb but for football fans who want to go back to their college towns for a weekend to watch a game. They rent a charming house instead of booking a crowded hotel—it's a sliver of a much bigger market, but it's a great niche and so smart. Like patrons of Rent Like a Champion, customers of challenger brands are attracted to companies willing to look over the horizon, discover what people need in the future, and then bring it to them ahead of schedule.

Another example of a brand that aims to change paradigms is TUSHY, a company that produces bidet attachments for toilets so, in their words, "your butt will be healthy like kale and clean like a toddler's vocabulary." As you can see, their marketing language is as refreshing as their product surely is. In a broader sense, they're changing paradigms by going into a category you'd think was untouchable, applying common sense to a common problem and challenging the status quo—a trait customers of challenger brands find very attractive.

SUMMARY

Now you know all about the customers your challenger brand needs to attract. They want to share their passion, be empowered to convert others, be rewarded in some way, and change paradigms by rejecting how things have always been done. What can your brand do to meet those expectations? Start by finding your shhhh.

WHAT'S YOUR SHHHH?

Some of the most successful brands, both big and small, share their best benefits with a select few. Finding your shhhh means finding that special something you don't overly promote in a traditional sense—the secret sauce—and giving it all the power. It's all about inclusive exclusivity. In the end, your shhhh can help you potentially steal customers from the Goliaths of your industry.

Strategic product offerings, for example, are an excellent way for challenger brands to begin because they can spur a grassroots marketing campaign or—at the very least—foster a loyal fan base. Ever ordered an off-menu item at your favorite restaurant and felt like a big shot? That's an example of you making a connection to a brand's shhhh and reveling in the air of prestige they created for you. Did you snap a photo of your plate and share it on Instagram along with a few hashtags? That's how brands can capitalize on their customers' social media clout.

Take In-N-Out Burger, for example—they're the greatest cultivator of inclusive exclusivity in the fast-food industry. First of all, they refused to expand beyond California's borders. When they finally agreed to broaden their horizon to other locations, they refused to franchise. Now, they're relatively easy to find all the way to Texas, my home state.

In-N-Out continues to maintain their challenger spirit by refusing to put their most popular items on their in-store menu. Things like protein style (where your favorite burger comes wrapped in lettuce instead of a carb-loaded bun) or animal style (your burger comes with their proprietary grilled onion spread) are apparent on their website, but they're not listed in-store. Walk up to the counter to order one, and you feel like you're a member of a secret society. That's their shhhh factor in action.

Now that the secret's out about In-N-Out, we have Stealth Starbucks to discuss. Despite being the world's largest coffee chain, Starbucks refuses to rest on its laurels. Totally aware that some espresso snobs wouldn't be caught dead supporting such a giant corporation, Starbucks took the offensive and began opening Stealth Starbucks locations. These stores are located in metropolitan areas around the country, and they smell and sound just like the shops where your local barista turns latte foam into fine art. If you take a closer look, you can see they're actually owned and operated by none other than Starbucks Corporation.

Another way Starbucks uses the power of its shhhh is by offering a short cup (if you know to ask). Most people think tall is the smallest size, but oftentimes hiding behind the counter is this eight-ounce vessel that's perfect for a true European-style latte—or hot chocolates for my daughters that are sized just right. Want more? Ask for a cotton-candy Frappuccino or a butter-beer latte. Walk out of there with one of those, and do you really think you could risk the temptation to tell someone you're carrying caffeine gold that's not even on the menu?

In the end, Starbucks is a perfect example of why, no matter how big your company gets, you should never lose your drive to challenge.

Airline company JetBlue's shhhh is that they're not stingy with their eats. What they may lack in legroom and destination choices, they make up for with free television, a free check-in bag, and unlimited snacks. On some airlines, you're lucky to get half a can of soda, but JetBlue will give you a six-pack of Coke and all the chips you can fit in your stomach. You just have to ask for it. Many new JetBlue passengers don't know this, though, because they're so accustomed to the traditional stinginess of the skies. It's JetBlue's shhhh—and just another way they deliver on their tagline "You above all."

Then there's Kimpton Hotels, a brand with sixty-four boutique hotels in thirty-two cities. No two locations are alike, but their continuity is their customer service. One way they've quietly built customer loyalty is by offering complimentary champagne and chocolate-covered strawberries. It doesn't matter whether it's a birthday, engagement, or honeymoon—all it takes is one mention to the concierge, and they'll see to it that your bedside table is garnished. Some locations across the country now even feature exclusive nightcap programs that feature port wine, brandy, cognac, and other spirits.

Finally, apparel company L.L. Bean has taken its shhhh to another level by offering a total 100 percent satisfaction guarantee. Have you owned your merchandise for a week? A century? It doesn't matter. If it fails to meet your needs, you can send it back for a refund or replacement, no questions asked. While other retailers are tightening the strings on their return policies, L.L. Bean's CEO, Steve Fuller, once told National Public Radio that the only concern he has is whether or not his company promotes the policy enough. Sure, there are some scammers out there, but L.L. Bean has also earned the trust of many consumers who are jaded by the increase in tedious return restrictions with other retailers. Their shhhh is all about building relationships.

In the age of social media where word-of-mouth recommendations hold even more weight than big flashy Super Bowl advertisements, it's in every brand's best interest to give the customers something to boast about. People are constantly looking for ways to make their lives sound more prestigious or interesting. If you give them a free bottle of champagne, unlimited Terra chips on a flight, or take their dirty old hiking boots back ten years after they were purchased, you'd better believe they're going to go to Instagram, Twitter, Snapchat, and Facebook to share the love.

☆ CHALLENGE YOURSELF ☆

WHAT'S YOUR DOUBLETREE COOKIE?

I was recently heading out the door on a business trip. As always, my daughters were milling around the kitchen, asking questions and politely feigning interest in my business meetings. Then, my oldest finally got to her point and asked, "Daddy, will you bring us back a present?" I told her I'd be in conference rooms most of the time, but I'd try. The next thing she said really stuck with me.

"Are you staying at a DoubleTree? If you are, can you bring us back a cookie?"

I was taken aback. In all my years of overseeing branding and campaign development for brands and even hotels, this was the first time a pint-sized human who can't even spell "reservation" was requesting something straight out of a marketer's playbook.

DoubleTree gives guests cookies. It's not a grand gesture, but it's a memorable one—one that matters. What's your DoubleTree cookie? What's your L.L. Bean return policy? What's on your secret menu?

Do some brand soul-searching, and come up with five small things your company could do to create advocacy, whether it's a product or an experience. Remember, what's small to you could actually be just the push your customers need to evolve into advocates.

EMPOWERED CHALLENGER TAKEAWAYS

As we conclude this chapter, you must remember these three points:

1. Without the advocacy of your customer, you can never successfully challenge. To gain that advocacy, you must first know your audience—I mean *really* know them.

2. The fastest-growing brands are turning predictability inside out while opting in to the idea that consumers control the message in this social, digital age.

3. There are four characteristics of an empowered challenger brand's customer—that is, your ideal customer if you're on the path to challenge. They want to share their passion, convert others, be rewarded, and change paradigms. Your brand must not only allow *but also enable* these tendencies.

☆ ☆ ☆ ☆ ☆

THE FIVE PERSONALITY TRAITS OF EMPOWERED CHALLENGERS

☆ ☆ ☆ ☆ ☆

LIGHTNING IN A BOTTLE

Being honest may not get you many friends but it'll always get you the right ones.

JOHN LENNON

The lightning-rod personality is one of the five traits your brand can leverage to topple your giants. When skies begin to darken and the thunder starts to crack, photographers point their lenses at lightning rods. Why? Their purpose is to conduct energy, and the resulting photo is often alluring and unforgettable.

Lady Gaga is a prime example of the personification of the lightning-rod personality. It wasn't about the meat dress—it was about doing something unexpected. Love her or hate her, you'll never forget her. While artists like Taylor Swift have won over millions of fans with radio-friendly songs about young love and breakups, Lady Gaga cultivated an army of what she called "little monsters"—a term for embracing all the things that make preachers and parents toss and turn in their sleep.

Gaga hasn't shied away from struggle, either. She became a beacon for acceptance for the LGBT community while taking darts from everyone from animal-rights activists to the NRA. By attacking both disciples and critics with her outrageousness, she's amassed over sixty-four million Twitter followers. Whether they're favoriting, retweeting, or trolling her account, they're paying attention. Couple that with the nearly one million people who have joined her "little monsters" fan page, and there's no denying the power of influence Gaga has garnered from her lyrics to her larger-than-life persona.

Outside of the pop-music sphere, take a look at Elon Musk. Here's the man bringing energy kicking and screaming into the twenty-first century. His message is simple and powerful: change the world and humanity by reducing global warming and using sustainable energy. Oh, and maybe make life multiplanetary by colonizing Mars. No big deal.

Lofty goals? Yes. Like it or not, though, you can't deny that Elon Musk has made society think twice about the way we power our cars, our homes, and even our countries. Believe him or debunk him, but he's moving forward anyway with his vision he aims to achieve through companies like Tesla Motors, SpaceX, and Solar City. Like any good lightning rod, he attracts a high concentration of both supporters and haters. For every Tesla fan who considers him the second coming of Edison, there's another who believes he's a bubble of lofty ambitions destined to burst like one of his SpaceX rockets.

In the end, the only thing Lady Gaga and Elon Musk don't attract is apathy. They're conductors at their cores, the very definition of a lightning-rod personality.

WHAT IS A LIGHTNING-ROD BRAND?

Brands that embody the lightning-rod personality are different, magnetic, and honest. You'll never find a lightning-rod brand following the herd or doing things for the sake of pleasing the majority. In other words, they don't drive a beige minivan, and they don't eat at Olive Garden.

Instead, they do just the opposite, and they do it unabashedly. They're the ones making you laugh or cry by tapping into core human truths. They're the types that show up unannounced at open-mic night and absolutely kill it.

How do they get there, though? The lightning-rod metaphor isn't only a reflection or an output of the brand evolution—it goes further than that. It represents the entire fabric of their culture. They're opportunistic, tapped into their real-time culture, and—here's a big one—willing to take calculated risks. In fact, this personality trait is typically born out of tension uncovered by and tapping into shared emotions or frustrations. That conflict is where the energy lives. That conflict is a cultivator. Every great drama, comic book, or TV show has conflict at the core, and finding your villain is the first step. Because creativity often happens in response to a problem, starting here can help lead your brand to harness its true, magnetic personality.

That's not the only way lightning-rod brands get ahead. They succeed in part by generating shareable content, using new-age media to their advantage. They're right at home in the digital landscape where Twitter posts spread like wildfire and blog posts outpace old-school news cycles.

"

LIGHTNING RODS ARE OPPORTUNISTIC, TAPPED INTO THEIR REAL-TIME CULTURE AND WILLING TO TAKE CALCULATED RISKS.

"

REAL-LIFE LIGHTNING-ROD CAMPAIGNS AND COMPANIES

The **Girls Who Code campaign** is gender's lightning rod, if you will. Walk around the engineering department of your average tech start-up, and you'll notice a lot of stand-up desks and half-consumed lattes. What you won't see, though, is a surplus of women, and Girls Who Code is a campaign that attempted to answer why. They released a video full of reasons women are so underrepresented in the world of software development, making wildly inappropriate, satirical statements like, "My menstrual cycle makes it so that I just can't code." In the end, the video was making the point that gender stereotypes in the workplace are equally as ridiculous.

In true lightning-rod fashion, the YouTube video got both fan and hate mail. Disapproval and praise came in virtual waves to their channel. Some commenters—mostly men—criticized the video, but others applauded it for bringing attention to a substantial societal problem. Either way, it blew up on YouTube in just a few short months, all the while reminding everyone that women are capable of remarkable things. Girls Who Code made their point by using humor and candor. Indeed, they were both polarizing *and* truthful, just what it took to get noticed in an industry that needs a bit of a wake-up call.

There is not one mold that produces a lightning-rod brand.

Rather, they come in all shapes and sizes. Here's proof:

- **#CocksnotGlocks** is an incarnation of what has always been the endearing weirdness of the University of Texas campus. We were all reminded of it when a group of students decided to protest Texas's passed campus carry law, making it legal for students to carry firearms from dorms to dining halls. To fight "absurdity with absurdity," hundreds of students opted to strap large, attention-grabbing prosthetic phalluses—dildos, as they're more commonly known—to their backpacks. Why? The message was clear: you can get in more trouble for openly carrying your sex toy than your side arm. Although the law remains the same, the protest generated enough lightning to catch the eyes of media outlets all over the world. Everyone from NRA members to anti-gun activists watched, enthralled. While the country is still far off from reaching a consensus on gun regulation, it's encouraging to know a small group of passionate crusaders can stir up conversation simply by getting creative. In a not-so-subtle, hilarious way, #CocksnotGlocks made a big point about a big issue.

- **Thinx** is a brand that turned the topic of a women's menstrual cycle on its head, taking it from taboo subject to the subject of a well-orchestrated marketing plan. Thinx is period panties—plain, simple, and unapologetically. They don't demonstrate their product by pouring blue Windex over a maxi pad or having a woman frolic around donning a pair of white skinny jeans and a perma-smile. Rather, they incorporate truthful portraits of people who have gone through their period and who use Thinx products, using language so honest that it has disrupted an industry. Why does it work? Thinx knows their audience, and they're not targeting the older person who might be offended or the young teenage boy who might scoff at the subject. They went after it, and they did it in true lightning-rod fashion.

- **Dumb Ways to Die** was a memorable campaign that made the concept of train safety decidedly unboring by adding humor and irreverence. At its core was an animated video out of Melbourne featuring hilarious, lovable characters and a catchy tune. The goal of the campaign was to encourage passengers to keep their distances from train tracks and generally be smart about train safety. Traditionally, you'd think a team of transit entities and government agencies would have gone with something heartfelt, buttoned-up, and conservative—however, they did the opposite. The video went through many ridiculous ways a human could die—including sticking your head in honey and walking up to a beehive—and argued they were equally as ridiculous as getting hit by a moving train. The result was a highly awarded campaign with global popularity and, most importantly, a giant downtick in railway accidents and near misses following its debut.

- **Axe**, a personal hygiene product from Unilever, is known for making males irresistible with a mere spray. They called it the "Axe Effect." Targeting fifteen- to twenty-five-year-old men,

> the premise of the Axe Effect campaign was to project the body spray as a nasal aphrodisiac in ways that were irreverent and edgy. In one commercial in particular, a man sprays himself with Axe body spray on the beach. Suddenly, attractive, bikini-clad women start coming out of the jungle and across the beach like herds of water buffalo. While occasionally controversial, Unilever's approach came straight from research about *why* men groom the way we do and the emotions behind those actions. The Axe Effect campaign broke down doors in what has become a multibillion-dollar grooming industry.

The Dallas Stars are a Texas-sized example of not only overcoming but also embracing the ultimate challenge of position. They are a hockey team in the thick of football country, after all. To build buzz around their upcoming season, they enlisted the help of Door Number 3. Our overarching goals were to distinguish the hockey experience from all other pro sports, activate the casual fan to come watch a game in person, and ignite personality around the brand. The stakes were high—the Stars share a building with the NBA's Dallas Mavericks and are right down the street from "America's Team," the NFL's Dallas Cowboys. With mindshare a challenge, we gave them the lightning-rod personality and created the "Come into the Cold" campaign.

Come into the Cold served up a spirited alternative to

comparatively tame football and basketball alternatives. We were focusing on what made hockey different. Campaign headlines included these: "Only One Game a Week? "Is the N in NFL for Nancy?" and "Ultimate Fighting. What a Friendly Little Sport." Our headline to promote opening night read: "Blood Drive Begins October 5th." Within 24 hours of its release, it became one of the most talked about campaigns in NHL history. Come into the Cold created a national dialog, and was featured on highly visible channels from ESPN's Around the Horn to the *New York Times.*

But why?

Part of it was the campaign itself, and part of it was harnessing the lightning rod's ability to be opportunistic. You see, in the middle of the Stars' season, their neighbors and Mark Cuban's baby, the Dallas Mavericks, got swept into the controversy of the NBA's point-shaving scandal. In short, referees were accused of shaving points to influence the outcome of games.

We got after it, immediately posting a giant outdoor board outside of the Stars' arena reading, "The only thing our refs shave is the ice. Dallas Stars: Come into the Cold." We knew we would ruffle feathers. We also knew Mark Cuban would drive by the board every day—but, knowing that some of the best creativity is born of conflict, we did it anyway.

It worked. The airwaves lit up, and Mark saw it. The next day in the *Dallas Morning News,* he was quoted as saying, "I think it's hysterical. Good for them." Come into the Cold was done for a distinct purpose, and the outdoor board was done in good fun but also to contribute to that purpose. It's an example of being a lightning rod, ready to be contextually relevant when there's an opportunity and to jump in headfirst.

☆ CHALLENGE YOURSELF ☆

WHAT'S YOUR MEAT DRESS?

Your brand can begin to incorporate the traits of the lightning-rod personality by going through the fun exercise of taking a giant step back. Be completely truthful about *who you are* and *why you are*, and leave the puffery and buzzwords at home. Then, take it even further and ask the same questions about your competitors.

Here's a fun way to look at it. Pretend Amy Schumer is doing a roast—first on you, and then on your top two competitors. What would she say? This isn't an exercise you're going to share with everyone on your website, but it *is* an exercise that forces you through some self-reflection. Ask yourself: "How can we be unabashed? How can we use humor? How can we be polarizing in a way that underscores what we're all about in a meaningful way, not just for the sake of shock value?"

To that end, if the blogosphere has taught us anything, it's that no topic is free of controversy. Would you rather sit on the sidelines and wait for the storm to go by, or would you prefer to raise your lightning rod in an effort to reach audiences on both sides of the fence? Yes, you might gain an enemy or two, but isn't that what being a lightning rod is all about? Being an empowered challenger is about taking calculated risks.

It's about more than that, too. Remember, this is only one stone. You've got four more. You don't have to wear a meat dress every day, but you need to be able to recognize that there might be a time and place for it. Take a stab at finding yours, and wear it proudly when the time is right.

EMPOWERED CHALLENGER TAKEAWAYS

As we conclude this chapter, you must remember these three points:

1. The lightning-rod personality is typically born out of tension because this tension is where the energy lives. This leads to a magnetic, honest personality that sets brands apart.

2. You'll never find a lightning-rod brand doing things for the sake of pleasing the majority.

3. Lightning rods come in all shapes and sizes, from #Cocksnot Glocks at the University of Texas to the Come into the Cold campaign for the Dallas Stars. The trick is finding the sweet spot that represents your brand.

LIGHTNING ROD

THINX

Miki Agrawal, Co-Founder & SHE E-O, Thinx

Thinx is a brand that set out to change the status quo about how women handle their periods, selling absorbent underwear that eliminate the need for traditional tampons or maxipads. Their marketing has an unfiltered, call-it-like-it-is quality that is refreshing in a market previously dominated by "period correctness" and actresses prancing around in white pants. In addition to their fresh product and even fresher approach, Thinx donates some funds from sales to a grassroots organization in Kampala—AFRIpads, to be exact—that focuses on sustainment, empowerment, and employment of women in Uganda. Cofounder and She-EO Miki Agrawal launched Thinx in January 2014, and it has embodied the lightning-rod personality ever since. How did Thinx do it? Below is my interview with Miki.

Q: Why is the lightning rod personality more the exception than the rule?

A: People are used to the status quo. And the status quo of the last hundred years has been "use a blue liquid, use a girl prancing in the field, talk about periods like it's the most wonderful thing in the world—when it's really not." If you're a company like P&G and you're making a lot of money, you don't want to change things and risk fucking up what you have. So it allows challenger brands like ours to really innovate.

Q: Thinx is an unabashed, unfiltered brand. As such, how do you know when you're crossing the line?

A: I don't think there's a line. Our whole thing is to just be exactly who we are and be unapologetic about it. If you talk about something unapologetically, if you talk about something without embarrassment, then all of the sudden there's nothing to be embarrassed about. We've been able to have very real conversations that people are dying to have. We are liberating people. I don't think being too bold and open with what's real goes too far. It's refreshing.

Q: What were your biggest hurdles when you first conceived of Thinx?

A: If you are addressing taboos, that in itself is a huge hurdle to climb over. The period taboo was our biggest challenge to overcome because nobody wants to talk about it. Every time there's a man in the room, girls get red in the face and guys get uncomfortable. We had to get over that. The year 2015 was our big period feminist movement. We definitely led that. I realized that in order to change culture and get people talking about it, there needs to be three very distinct components.

The first component is you have to have an innovative product to break a taboo. It can't be half-assed innovation. It has to be something that is truly revolutionary that people want to use.

The second part to change culture in our category is considered, artful design across every touch point of our brand: our postcards, our packaging, our website, our Facebook ads, our out-of-home campaigns. We consider very carefully the artfulness and design elements of our brand. When someone is walking through a subway station and sees our ad, they think, *Wow, what a beautiful ad.* And then they think, *It doesn't even look like an ad—it looks like a piece of art.* And then they look closer, and we're talking about periods, and they're like, *Whoa, whoa!* They think, *I can't deny that it's beautiful.* And that helps open up that dialogue.

The third component to changing culture is accessible, relatable communication. If we're talking about something technical or academic, we could be very clinical about what we're doing. Instead, the way we write and the way we talk is like we're texting our best girlfriend. It feels familiar. You can relate to it. It's like I'm talking to you like a friend, not like an advertisement. All three components together really do transform culture.

Q: For every pair of underwear Thinx sells, you fund the production of seven washable cloth pads for girls in developing countries. How important is social entrepreneurship to your business model? And are you concerned that entrepreneurs are beginning to leverage the giveback model as more of a marketing tactic than a genuine core philosophy?

A: The future of entrepreneurship is social entrepreneurship. I think it's a buzzword when it's used for marketing. I don't think it's a buzzword when it's used authentically. I don't think there's anything wrong with incorporating a giveback if it really is authentic to you. It falls apart when people think they need to find a giveback for marketing purposes. When people tell me that they want to incorporate a giveback, I ask, "So what do you really care about?"

Interestingly, a lot of our audience doesn't even know about our model. It's only mentioned at the bottom of our website. Some companies do this for marketing. The one-for-one model has been done so many times now, it feels a little bit disingenuous. So we just did our own model. When people discover it, they think, "Wow, that's beautiful."

We're launching our Global Girls Club under our Thinx Foundation in 2017. We've developed a six-month curriculum. At the end of six months, these girls will get hard cash to start businesses. We're launching this all around the world. These are the stories we want to tell. For example, a girl in Nepal living in a cow shed with no prospects and no possibilities can join the Global Girls Club, and in six months she can start a business and she's out of her shitty situation. That's what we're going to do across the world for girls. This will be built into the Thinx model. For every pair of underwear sold, we'll be helping a girl to get out of her current situation.

Q: What has been your toughest lesson since launching Thinx?

A: The hiring process is really hard. The partnership process often doesn't work out between two people. It's so important, when you think about a cofounder or a partner, that they have exact opposite skill sets to you. So if I'm branding, creative, design, PR, I need someone who's awesome at operations, finance, manufacturing, and product development. When you bring someone on who's a friend, and they want to do what you want to do, it hurts business. The thing I would do over again is really hire slow and fire fast. I won't make that mistake again.

LET'S GET HERETICAL

Get closer than ever to your customers. So close, in fact, that you tell them what they need well before they realize it themselves.

STEVE JOBS

Brands that embody a heretical point of view excel at looking over the horizon and bringing consumers something they didn't even know they needed. Not only that, but they do it ahead of schedule. **Heretical brands excel at redefining perspectives and, in the process,**

have recognized that comparing themselves to their competition is the same as comparing themselves to mediocrity.

THE CASE FOR THE HERETICAL BRAND

Since 2011, more than $18 billion in market share shifted to small to midsized brands, which now accounts for nearly half of all US consumer product goods sales. Consumers are voting with their wallets, making it clear that there's no better time for heretics to take risks and blaze new trails. These brands are becoming today's marketplace victors.

An example of a brand that embodies a heretical perspective is Revolution Foods, an Oakland-based company that makes school lunches that are junk-free, freshly prepared, and locally made—all while staying within public school districts' ultra-tight budgets. Revolution Foods is now a $150 million business with two thousand employees. Today, it operates in 1,600 schools, and its packaged meals sell in grocery stores in forty-four states and on major e-commerce sites like Amazon.

It's clearly a successful company, but why is Revolution Foods heretical? It comes down to their purpose and perspective, as they battled bureaucracy and complacency to come to market and grow. The business was started by two moms and MBA graduates, Kristin Groos Richmond and Kirsten Saenz Tobey, in a small kitchen in Oakland, California. Frustrated by the dry, cardboard-tasting pieces of hormone-injected chicken and the like that children were being fed at school, they took it upon themselves to fix it.

With the help of a few friends, they worked through the nights prepping and packaging all-natural spaghetti, meat-balls, carrots, fresh peaches, and more—no additives, no artificial colors, no preservatives. These two women took it upon themselves to change an entire system. Kristin and Kirsten did the cooking. They worked on packaging. They drove the truck, delivering meals to schools to prove their concepts and get funding.

Revolution Foods grew from there, and for good reason. Like many of you, I grew up eating poor cafeteria food. It took too long for us to realize how the quality of the food we serve in schools affects the energy levels of our children, not to mention their appetites for education. Through bravery and hard work, though, Revolution Foods set out to change the game.

There was also sacrifice, which again speaks to their heretical spirit. Kristin found out she was pregnant with her first child right in the middle of the company's development.

People told her to graduate, to just take a break from the business, and have her baby. Start the company later.

She didn't.

At that time, the obesity epidemic was growing, and Kristin felt this pull. She went to talk to her graduate-school mentor, Kellie McElahney, about her business and her fears. She remembers Kellie leaning across that desk and saying, "Whatever you do, do not quit. You can do this. If you go for this and follow your passion, you're actually going to be a *better parent* in the long run because you're going to be inspired and fulfilled, and you can pass that along to your kids." Kristin recalls it as a pivotal moment that reinvigorated her entrepreneurial spirit and propelled her forward.

Netflix is another example of a heretical company, a very recognizable example of a brand focused on giving customers what they need before they can even ask. Netflix started with mail-order DVDs. Led by CEO Reed Hastings, they've branched into streaming shows and even producing their own content. In a way, it has become the standard for how people watch television, racking up over eighty-three million users and a value of over $32.9 billion—more than the entire CBS network.

The CEO of Blockbuster, John Antioco, actually had the chance to purchase Netflix for a mere $50 million in 2000, but he declined Hastings' offer because he felt the business had too narrow of a niche. At the time, Netflix was just a DVD mailing service, and he didn't see the vision.

What Antioco missed is clear today: the future of the video market is no longer built of brick and mortar. Today's customer demands something more. While Antioco's team was probably preoccupied putting those "Be Kind, Rewind" stickers on VHS tapes, Netflix was honing their heretical side and finding new ways to deliver value to consumers. In 2010, Blockbuster filed for bankruptcy when it lost $1.1 billion. In comparison, 37 percent of the Internet bandwidth during peak hours is now devoted to Netflix streaming.

WHY A HERETICAL PERSONALITY WORKS WELL FOR BRANDS

Remember how customers of challenger brands want to change paradigms? A heretical personality works so well because customers often have a deep attachment not only to the product or service but also to the message. In fact, consumers are encouraged to align with a heretical brand's vision and be a part of their higher calling. This doesn't come easily, though—**being truly heretical takes**

bravery, sacrifice, and an innovative spirit. That's what sets heretical brands apart from their competition.

A brand built on such bravery is EPIC Provisions. Founded in 2013 by Katie Forrest and Taylor Collins, EPIC is a company that entered a hot nutrition-bar category with a product packed with meaty goodness for the paleo-minded. EPIC was born out of Katie and Taylor's own need to have an accessible paleo snack that fit their diet and lifestyle. Although they believed their product had appeal, they had to deal with naysayers throughout their early days. Skeptics would ask, "Are you guys still working on that *meat* bar?" They pressed on, though, to eventually break into the market in a big way. EPIC moved nimbly, built a fan base, and sold to General Mills in early 2016. When you can't beat 'em, buy 'em.

Yvon Chouinard, founder of Patagonia, once said during an interview with National Public Radio, "If you wait for your customer to tell you what to do, you're too late." Indeed, Katie and Taylor's story embodies this very advice. The lesson? Stay out front, bravely innovate, and never miss an opportunity to stand on a chair and peer over the horizon.

THE HERETICAL CUSTOMER EXPERIENCE

A heretical personality can show up in many ways, be that product development, brand messaging, or the customer experience. Lemonade, a Culver City-based restaurant, is an example of the customer experience being redefined.

Where I'm from, when someone says "cafeteria food," I think Luby's or Furr's. Grab a tray, reluctantly reach for the shaved beets, take a slab of chicken fried steak, and slide a wiggly scoop of gelatin dessert onto your tray.

Lemonade said, "To hell with all of that." They took something familiar and turned it on its head. They revitalized the staid cafeteria experience with bright locations serving fresh, California cuisine. Charming interiors replaced the drab wall-to-wall cafeteria carpet we were all accustomed to. Lemonade's fanatical following has led to growth as sweet as its signature lemonade, with twenty-four locations to date.

Like Lemonade, heretical brands succeed when it comes to differentiation, and they know how to identify clear propositions. This brand confidence starts with a higher calling and is manifested with the help of a strong power of belief. With heretical brands, it's almost impossible to disconnect the vision of the brand's leader—think of Kristin and Kirsten of Revolution Foods, Jeff Bezos of

Amazon, or Tony Hsieh of Zappos. They reinvented customer service and changed industries by making the world around them a better place.

Then there's Austin-born Daily Greens, an innovative company born out of pure necessity. Shauna Martin, the founder of Daily Greens, started the company after she became more conscious of her nutrient intake while battling breast cancer. So she started making herself an organic green juice every day. The results were phenomenal. Not only did she recover very quickly from her two-year battle with cancer, but she also had more energy and stamina than ever before. Shauna was convinced that she had discovered the fountain of youth, but the problem was the time and money involved in making an organic green juice, which usually involves thirty to forty minutes of prep and cleanup and over ten dollars of organic produce. Most folks, including Shauna, did not have the income or patience to do this on a daily basis. She founded Daily Greens with the goal of making the most nutrient-dense, organic green juice on the market, and making it available and affordable so that everyone can drink one every day. It's impossible to disconnect her strong power of belief—or herself—from her strongly heretical business.

A heretical brand approaches everything differently, even

marketing. They require high-impact advertising that draws people in. Often, it's experiential and participatory. Heretical companies want their consumers off the sidelines and engaged with their mission. Remember the lightning-rod brands? They might make you laugh or stir up water-cooler conversation with their flavor of marketing, but it's something else with heretical brands. They need to dig a little deeper and grab audiences at the visceral level.

THE HERETICAL STORYTELLER

If you're a brand with a heretical personality, your mode of storytelling can't be served up on stale rye toast. Like the product itself, it must be innovative.

BMW doesn't just make the Ultimate Driving Machine. They've been known to engineer the Ultimate Ad Campaign. The BMW film series, *The Hire*, was a series of eight short films (averaging about ten minutes each) produced as Internet films in 2001 and 2002. The shorts were directed by popular filmmakers from around the world and starred Clive Owen as "The Driver" going from place to place in BMWs. With this, BMW pioneered a new form of branded content that until then had never been done before. They created a form of storytelling that was as future-focused as what's under their hood.

A more recent example of this is when Old Spice developed an interactive campaign to capitalize on the popularity of the "Old Spice Guy." The result was an Old Spice "response" campaign—an experiment in real-time branding featuring the Old Spice character posting personal video responses to fans. Nearly two hundred video messages were deployed across social networks in just two days of filming. The campaign went on to record tens of millions of views, making it one of the most memorable and innovative interactive campaigns in history. Old Spice didn't just look over the horizon and bring us into a world where all men believed they needed to achieve legendary status by lathering up with soapy goodness. They also found a way to reinvent how customers interact with brands.

Note that it's not only big brands like Amazon with their drone delivery system that are winning with a heretical personality scorecard. Take a look at Silvercar, a company that has travelers conveniently renting silver Audi A4s at the airport through an app on their smartphone. That's not all, though—they also gave us a whole new perspective about the car rental experience. People were frustrated, tired of rental car roulette and a routinely poor experience. In true challenger fashion, Silvercar set out to shift paradigms for their audience. Every Audi you get from them will smell like leather, not the leftover smells

“

YOUR MODE OF STORYTELLING CAN’T BE SERVED UP ON STALE RYE TOAST. LIKE THE PRODUCT ITSELF, IT MUST BE INNOVATIVE.

”

from the last renter. No waiting, no line, no wondering. It's concierge-like customer service, and it works.

The likes of Revolution Foods, EPIC, and Silvercar aren't the only heretical champions. Here's proof:

- **Glock:** A heretical approach often starts with the product itself. As an example of heretical manufacturing, look no further than Gaston Glock. Glock started his career as a curtain-rod maker. He had no experience with gun manufacturing, but he had a deep knowledge of plastics, and like all good heretics, he saw a gap in the marketplace in the firearm industry. He asked gun experts in his native Austria what could be done to improve a handgun for the modern era and went on to make a prototype based on their feedback. The result: the original Glock 17, a lightweight, durable, and reliable gun—with a larger ammunition capacity—that could be easily learned, fired, and even submerged in water or subjected to high heats without failing. Its engineering was inspired by the process of manufacturing curtain rods!

- **Peloton:** Of course, the most heretical companies don't always invent from scratch. They take something that already exists and make it better. I have a good friend who is an avid cyclist; he loves racing, loves riding hard, and loves outdoor adventure. But he's now approaching his mid-forties. Recovering from a spill isn't nearly as easy as it was when he was in his twenties. Those falls hurt a little more, and recovery takes twice as long. He told me about Peloton, a stationary bike he's considering purchasing for his home. This isn't that rusty exercise bike sitting in the corner of your bedroom that inevitably winds up becoming a place to drape your bath towel. Peloton has brought the spin craze right into peoples' homes by creating the only exercise machine to stream live cycling classes, so you can experience epic spin classes on your own schedule. It's indoor cycling completely reimagined. This innovation is projected to put the brand at $150 million in revenue.

☆ CHALLENGE YOURSELF ☆

WHAT CAN YOU LEARN FROM OUTSIDE INDUSTRIES?

Many brands can't shake that tugging tendency to compare themselves *only* to competitors in their market. Apparel companies look at apparel companies. Banks study other banks. You get the picture. Heretical companies do that and more, though, because they realize that comparing themselves solely to their direct competition only limits their potential.

Instead, heretical brands innovate by taking cues from entirely different industries. That apparel company, then, might also look at consumer-goods companies outside of the clothing industry. What are they doing well? What is there to learn from their approach?

This strategy is important for a number of reasons. First, it's proven through the history of successful critical thinkers. Russian inventor Genrikh Altshuller suggested that 95 percent of "new problems" have already been solved, most likely many times over. He believed that solutions to your own challenges are most likely to come from industries that you do not have firsthand knowledge about. Case in point? Henry Ford—you may have heard of him—borrowed manufacturing techniques common in the meatpacking industry and applied them to building cars.

Think about it this way: when you take ideas from within your own industry, you risk becoming a me-too. When you apply an idea from another industry and adapt it to your own, you create something remarkable. You drive innovation. And the greater the distance between industries, the greater the novelty of the solution.

To truly challenge your brand and get in the heretical spirit, pick an innovative company outside of your comfort zone, even half a world away. Write down five ideas for how their approach might translate to your business challenge. Look at everything—their customer service, their website, their packaging, their approach to social media content. How do they tell their story, and what can your brand learn from it? Finding inspiration from other categories is the ultimate heretical move.

EMPOWERED CHALLENGER TAKEAWAYS

As we conclude this chapter, you must remember these three points:

1. Heretical brands redefine perspectives by knowing what customers want before they do and delivering it ahead of schedule.

2. A heretical personality works well for brands because forward-thinking customers often have a personal attachment to their product or service. In fact, consumers are encouraged to align with a heretical brand's vision and be a part of their higher calling.

3. A heretical brand approaches everything differently, even marketing. They require high-impact advertising that draws people in. Experiential and participatory strategies work best.

HERETICAL

REVOLUTION FOODS

Left: Kristin Groos Richmond, Co-Founder & Chairman of the Board, Revolution Foods
Right: Kirstin Saenz Tobey, Co-Founder & Chief Impact Officer, Revolution Foods

Revolution Foods was founded by two moms—Kristin Groos Richmond and Kirsten Saenz Tobey—who had a simple yet powerful idea: they believed school lunches should be healthier. By pursing that passion, they have changed not only what today's schoolchildren eat but also how schoolchildren approach a healthy lifestyle, by promoting nutrition education and aiming to provide every child with access to quality food options that promote growth and development. The brand has expanded into retail stores and recently partnered with another company started by moms, Batter World, to add wholesome breakfast options to their family of products. By redefining perspectives and leading with purpose, Revolution Foods couldn't be more heretical. How'd they do it? Below is my interview with Kristin Groos Richmond, cofounder of Revolution Foods.

Q: For so long we've blindly accepted that cafeteria food will never be nutritious or delicious. Perhaps it was apathy, indifference, affordability, or some combination of all three. When the idea for Revolution Foods first came to you and Kirsten, what was the biggest obstacle that stood between you and a successful launch?

A: From the outset, we were very focused on access for all kids. Our real goal was to be able to bring healthy, delicious, fresh meals to kids every day—kids with the least amount of access. We knew affordability was going to be a big issue. Yet we had to stay true to high food standards to accomplish our mission. We wanted to replace processed microwavable food with real homemade meals. So we knew we had to focus on menu design through students to create a delicious product that kids loved. To accomplish this, we needed an incredibly high-quality supply chain that did not previously exist in K-12 meals.

Q: One ingredient can be the difference between a clean plate and a plate that goes untouched. Describe your approach for gathering feedback from your most precious (and fickle) audience.

A: We really started with our students. We started by creating meals in a pilot and taking feedback from students. Food is a very personal thing, and there are also key elements of cultural relevance to menus. We have an incredibly diverse group of students to serve across the country. So we had to really listen and design to the desires of the communities we serve. There's also a misconception with kids and food: the idea that kids love junk food. It's not true. Chicken nuggets that are partly frozen on the inside? Most students are saying they want better options. They said to us, "If you give me something that looks good, tastes good, I'd be very excited to eat it." Approaching the process with respect and true listening was how we tackled the challenge, and it's still what we do at the core. It's one of our pillars.

Q: Your company's mission isn't a boilerplate statement on the website. It's very personal to you and Kirsten, and the oxygen that fuels your growth. What have you done to ensure that every Revolution Foods staff member understands, lives, and breathes this mission?

A: We have very strong core values that guide the company. They're talked about constantly. They're visible in our culinary centers. They're talked about in our team huddles. We live the mission. And people come here because of the mission. It's one of the great things about building a mission-focused company. You attract people with a shared mind-set. It's a big recruiting tool actually, and it's all reinforced through our teams. I take the time to meet with people and conduct town-hall meetings around the country, but we also have a strong training program. We make sure our leadership at the local level is completely fluid talking about the mission. The mission has to live through our leadership at all levels in all regions.

Q: You've expanded from schools to grocery aisles. How did you know it was time? What key considerations went into that decision?

A: We knew early on that we would go in that direction. We've always been passionate about serving families as well as students. We just weren't sure of the timing. Parents came up to us and said that they would love to bring home our delicious lunch for dinner. Literally, "Can we bring these home?" When we had parents asking to bring home the school meals being served, we thought we should actually commercialize this concept. We also had retailers approach us saying that they're looking for more mission-driven brands. Revolution Foods is committed to building lifelong healthy eaters. We knew consumers would be very drawn to our mission.

Q: You and Kirsten endured some hardships to launch a "revolutionary" product, including packing up your young families and moving from the Bay Area to DC to get the fledgling school meal program off the ground. What advice would you give a forward-thinking entrepreneur who is blazing new trails and battling years of status quo?

A: Run a pilot. Lots of aspiring entrepreneurs spend a lot of time building a business plan. This can lead to analysis paralysis. The most important thing you can do is pilot your concept. We piloted our concept in Oakland. We got a real sense of what students actually thought of the food. How do we transport it? How do we think about supply chain? What do investors care about? You've got to get out of your head early on and figure out a way to get some real market experience and feedback as quickly as you can. Drafting the concept and building the model is important, but you're going to learn a great deal from piloting in the real world.

Also, remember that you're always fundraising. People often wait too long to get started. It's better to have this in mind early and build connections. Say you miss out on an opportunity in round one with an investor—that doesn't mean you won't get the opportunity to come back and build that relationship. Don't give up! Make a great impression, and keep people educated on your progress. They will end up becoming a partner or investor down the road. This has happened to me many times.

Q: What's a challenger attribute that sets you apart?

A: Our innovation from concept to shelf can be less than six months. That's fast. And this type of speed is a very important attribute for disruptors. It becomes harder as companies get bigger. Make sure you fuel that innovation machine.

Q: What's the one thing you wish you had known when you launched Revolution Foods?

A: Hire earlier than you think you should. As an entrepreneur, you're trying to manage cash and wearing a lot of hats. You make mistakes if you hire too slowly or hire replicas of yourself. You need to understand what a complimentary team composition looks like. Your team is everything. You have to be humble enough to know what you're good at and where you need experience or help. My advice is to hire earlier than you think you should. When you have a great team, that's when great things happen. And hire people who are not only incredibly talented but also passionate about your mission. This will keep them committed through the ups and downs of company building!

Q: If you could have one do-over, what would it be?

A: There are a lot of those things. I learn a lot more from failure than success. I believe in reflecting on our missteps and not making the same mistake twice. When building a company, you make a lot of mistakes—like a menu going off track because you didn't take in all the feedback, little things like that. We also scaled quickly in certain regions and didn't have the right operational team in place early enough. We could have laid the foundation to scale better. I've been reflecting a lot lately. At the end of the day, we're now tracking toward $150 million in revenue with two thousand employees. It's been an amazing journey!

I DON'T WANT YOU; YOU WANT ME

If anyone can have it, I don't want it.

UNKNOWN

Fostering rejection is another tool in the empowered challenger's playbook, and it is all about the art of rejecting the masses in order to attract your most ardent fans. Does that mean your brand should strive for rejection? No, of course not—but it *does* mean you should stop being afraid of it. Think of your own circle of friends, for example. There have been multiple studies that have found you cannot have a meaningful relationship with more than a certain number of people. The numbers vary by study, but the point is the same: be choosy. When you surround yourself with too many people, it dilutes your potential for true connection.

If we're being honest with ourselves, we all have friends who just don't fit into our lives. They're flaky. They're emotionally draining. We have nothing in common with them. They encourage us to make bad decisions. Yet, we still meet them for happy hour, go to their kids' birthday parties, or double-tap their Instagram posts. Why? We know we might be wasting critical time and energy that could be focused on lasting friendships that feed our souls and help us grow, but we're just a little too afraid that our social stock might drop if we cut them off. How would it make us look? What might would we miss out on if we defriended them, both online and off?

Some brands feel the same way, except their huge social circles actually comprise their target audience, and that's a problem. They'll continue to spend marketing dollars to attract the wrong kinds of friends—ahem, customers—and they do so without remorse. In fact, they're proud of it, running to the C-suite every quarter with a presentation full of charts and dashboards that illustrate that the potential friendship market for their company is exponential.

Except it's not—at least, it shouldn't be. Empowered challengers looking to reshape old business models shouldn't have something for everyone, and they shouldn't try to attract everyone. After all, why would you call it a "target" audience when you're targeting, well, every consumer? These businesses are burning daylight with hangers-on when they should be bonding with the loyal people who love them the most. Over time, they will actually gain widespread popularity because their initial growth strategy catered to their most passionate zealots.

Enter brands that foster rejection, the complete opposites of those overly friendly brands. **Companies that embrace this challenger trait practice inclusive exclusivity. They're not afraid to lose fans.** They push away the masses and focus on pleasing a select few, confident in the knowledge that those who stick around will popularize their brand in a more meaningful and sustainable way.

Take, for example, Tough Mudder—an endurance event that that consists of a ten- to twelve-mile-long run, complete with a military-style obstacle course. It was designed and created by a British Harvard Business School postgraduate and former corporate lawyer. The event tests both physical and mental strength, and obstacles are so intense that they can even include electroshock therapy.

When Tough Mudder first dipped its toe into the muddy waters of endurance races, was it for everyone? No, absolutely not—and they didn't pretend to be, either. In fact, Tough Mudder is *happily the wrong fit* for those unwilling to pull, push, and will their ways through obstacles like the Blackness Monster, a sixty-foot slick of rotating barriers. The brand has become widely successful because they honed in on a very singular passion point, catered to an audience of die-hards who believe in it, and set the table for these athletes to spread the word over and over, thus attracting a wider audience over time. This kind of unbridled fanaticism is a hard thing to achieve, but it's a testament to the power of customers being in control of the message—and, when they care, they feel like it's their message, too. Brands that foster rejection as well as Tough Mudder do just that—they cultivate an audience that cares instead of pandering to everyone for clicks and shares.

Tough Mudder isn't the only champion of fostering rejection. Here's proof:

- **Benetton:** I grew up being repeatedly wide-eyed by the advertisements coming from this apparel company. They wanted it that way, though, and it was certainly a memorable approach. I saw world leaders kissing, a giant advertisement of a topless African American woman breast-feeding a Caucasian infant—you get the picture. Benetton was ahead of their time in a lot of ways, and one of those ways was how they dialed in to their biggest fan base who appreciated their unique approach to storytelling.

- **Christian Louboutin:** In 1992, French footwear designer Christian Louboutin felt like his shoes lacked something. Inspired by the Chanel nail polish an employee was wearing, he applied red-lacquered soles to his shoes, making them instantly recognizable. There's another aspect to Louboutin's shoes that make them recognizable, and that's the price tag. This is a brand that basically prices people out of contention, fostering rejection and building a tribe of well-off, red-soled customers in the process.

- **Patagonia:** Meet the outdoor gear and clothing business that wants you to think twice before buying their product. It's Patagonia's philosophy that it's better to purchase a few well-made jackets that you keep forever than to purchase a slew of poorly made jackets that will ultimately end up in a landfill. As part of this philosophy, Patagonia owns and operates the largest garment-repair facility in North America. They repair Patagonia products—no matter how long you've owned them. They'll even repair garments that *aren't* Patagonia because, in their mind, it's their obligation as a manufacturer to share the good word of sustainable consumption. In a world where so many companies desperately offer door-busting deals to get you to swipe your credit card and keep consuming, Patagonia takes an entirely different tack by saying: "Don't buy what you don't need. Think twice before you buy anything."

- **Hendrick's Gin:** Soccer mom? Lightweight? Prefer a PBR beer to a hoppy microbrew or a well drink to the pricier aged whiskey hidden in the back? Sorry, but Hendrick's Gin doesn't want you, and they even put it on the bottle: "It's not for everyone." It's admittedly an exclusionary brand, and its product is not meant to appeal to the masses. Does everyone love the approach? Certainly not—but lots of people do, and Hendrick's has built a fierce fan base out of them.

THE VALUE OF BEING A MANGO AMONG APPLES

Excelling at fostering rejection means being a mango among apples and liking the tree you're in. It goes back to looking around your category and taking advantage of the opportunities to really define and exploit a blindingly clear point of differentiation.

Dollar Shave Club is a mango in an industry with a whole lot of apples. They didn't enter the marketplace with dreams of appealing to everyone with unwanted body hair—which, let's face it, really is everyone at one point or another. Instead, they worked on setting themselves apart from the sea of mediocrity that is the world of razor companies. For decades, we were shown animated advertisements of blades sliding across our chins, and nobody even thought to do anything differently—until Dollar Shave Club.

They came on the scene aiming to appeal to young men—dude-bros, if you will—who were tired of paying top dollar for disposable blades. Who were tired of going into Walgreens and having to ask the cashier to come unlock a Plexiglas case just so they could tend to the laborious chore of basic hygiene. Who were over the old routine of paying for terrible, overpriced razors—and somehow still always running out.

So, they fixed it. They mixed mail-order affordability with attitude, and they grew enormously in just five years. Guess where they are now? The little challenger with the hysterical viral video sold to Unilever for a whopping one billion dollars. They're another example of "when you can't beat 'em, buy 'em"—because that's exactly what happened in the case of giant Unilever and empowered challenger Dollar Shave Club.

Dollar Shave Club succeeded, in part, because they discovered how to release their inner remarkability. Yuengling, a well-known Pennsylvania beer, is another brand that has done the same. Fans used to trek across the Ohio–Pennsylvania state line to buy cases of their super-beloved yet super-hard-to-get brew. When something is hard to get, there becomes a bit of fanaticism around it, and that's what happened to Yuengling. CrossFit is another good example of inner remarkability leading to fanaticism. CrossFit isn't just a hell of a good workout; it's a lifestyle and community. The number of CrossFit gyms in the United States grew 1900 percent in the first six years of the company. Enthusiasts will bend your ear talking about box jumps and deadlifts, and they've got the bumper stickers to prove it. While some hate it, for others, it is a religious experience.

I'm not the only one who sees it, either. Take El Arroyo, an iconic Tex-Mex restaurant in downtown Austin. It's been located on Fifth Street for decades, and they have a marquee up front. Every day, they post a funny headline to make people chuckle as they drive into downtown Austin. You can't miss it. There's always a headline that's fun and culturally relevant. One of my recent favorites read, "If a vegan does CrossFit, which do they talk about first?" It's funny because it's true. It gets right into the inner remarkabilities of each habit. There's something interesting about all these companies that foster rejection in one way or another: once people talk others into getting on board with the brand, activity, or lifestyle, it becomes a subculture that has serious word-of-mouth appeal.

Are Yuengling and CrossFit for everyone? Absolutely not. Have they each released their inner remarkability? Absolutely yes. These brands have been evangelized—much like being a vegan or wearing red-lacquered-soled shoes or reusing your Lululemon Athletica bag for your dry cleaning two months after your purchase—and have really excelled at tapping into creative conversations around their businesses.

Say your brand has vowed to foster rejection and is setting out to unleash your inner remarkability. Great! How can you do this well, creating a core fascination that fosters magnetism around your brand? First, you'll need to identify and evangelize what makes you special, and that starts with knowing where your biggest fans live—whether online or offline. Once you figure that out, you can spend all your time and resources giving them stories, insight, exclusive offers, and other content that gets them excited, arming them with the tools they need to spread the love. (Maybe print some bumper stickers, while you're at it. People love those. Seriously.)

What happens if you jump on the "something for everyone" train? You're bound to derail eventually. Just look at Radio Shack.

Need a remote-controlled monster truck? An indoor

antenna? How about hearing aid batteries? Radio Shack tried to mean everything to everyone until it eventually meant nothing. There's no bigger way to shoot yourself in the foot than to be nonfocused. Radio Shack is a brand that never fostered rejection, and it led to their demise. By reinventing itself, it could possibly live on after bankruptcy as long as the company remembers one thing that's simple to say yet difficult to do: differentiate your brand by identifying its biggest advocates, even at the risk of alienating others. There's a place for Walmarts and other one-size-fits-all stores, but we're now in a world where people gravitate to niche brands and specialty shops. You can't be both, so establish a consistent plan to deliver fascination to your truest advocates.

I touched on this earlier, but the menu at the Cheesecake Factory is another example worth mentioning here in the blacklisted "something for everyone" category. From cheesecake to crispy crab bites, they've got it. They may have been grandfathered in to this "to hell with specificity, we've got it all" strategy, but that doesn't mean it's infinitely sustainable. If you're going to be relevant today, whether in the restaurant industry or out of it, remember that long gone are the days when swinging for the fence was the only way to win. Longer doesn't mean better. A bigger audience doesn't mean your brand is getting more love.

“

A BIGGER AUDIENCE DOESN’T MEAN YOUR BRAND IS GETTING MORE LOVE.

”

☆ CHALLENGE YOURSELF ☆

WHAT SMALL DOORS CAN YOU SHUT SO BIG ONES CAN OPEN?

Speaking of audience love—you want it, right? Of course you do. So, how can you nail down your overall audience in such a way that actually grows your devoted tribe? You must shut some doors—yes, probably more than one—with total confidence in order for that big door to open.

Start here: write down all your target audiences. Study the list, glide your fingers over the letters, play your special song, and maybe take them out of your pocket for one last drink. Then, say good-bye to all but one.

It's okay, it's okay—this is just a drill. For now, just *act* as if you're saying good-bye to all but one. How do you choose *the one*, though? Ask yourself: "Who is our greatest advocate?" With only their passion points in mind, jot down ten things you could do to appeal to them on a new level. Completely forget about the other audiences and how those decisions would affect—or even anger—them. Go through the entire customer journey with that one target in mind, thinking of ways you can dial up the passion and improve *only their* experience.

It's truly an enlightening exercise, even if you scale it back a bit. Maybe you decide to widen your audience again after going through the steps above, and that's okay. Say you started with six audiences. After going through the "only one audience" exercise, you decide there are really two more audience subsets that hold your truest advocates. Congratulations! You've now gotten rid of three hangers-on that were stifling your progress. Now, you can move forward by focusing on delivering fascination and an insane amount of value to your most loyal fans.

EMPOWERED CHALLENGER TAKEAWAYS

As we conclude this chapter, you must remember these three points:

1. Fostering rejection means rejecting the masses in order to attract your most ardent fans. It doesn't mean you should strive for rejection—but it *does* mean you must stop being afraid of it.

2. Your brand shouldn't have something for everyone, and you shouldn't try to attract everyone. After all, why would you call it a "target" audience when you're targeting, well, every consumer? Brands such as Dollar Shave Club and Tough Mudder have nailed this balancing act.

3. Staying consistent is a big part of fostering rejection. Staying true

to your brightest differentiators and steadfast in your mission to keep your brand fascinating isn't always easy, but it's worth it in the end.

FOSTER REJECTION

TOUGH MUDDER

Jerome Hiquet, Chief Marketing Officer, Tough Mudder Inc

With obstacles like the Birth Canal, Everest 2.0, King of the Swingers, and Shawshanked, Tough Mudder isn't for everybody. The race course consists of ten to twelve miles—although elites can travel up to one hundred miles in twenty-four hours—and is physically and mentally challenging. Tough Mudders emphasize teamwork and camaraderie, and while participants are timed, finishing is the point (not the pace). Although Tough Mudder has now gone on to host over two hundred events since 2010 and grown enough to feature a few events targeted to varying skill levels, its roots—those slippery, sweaty, strong roots—were able to thrive thanks to the success realized by fostering rejection and building a robust base of die-hard fans. According to its website, some ten thousand of those die-hard finishers have even felt called to get a Tough Mudder tattoo; that's saying something. How'd they do it? Below is my interview with Jerome Hiquet, chief marketing officer at Tough Mudder, Inc.

Q: Tough Mudder attracts droves of fans around a very specific passion point. When the company was first founded, was there any concern that the Tough Mudder offering might be too narrow?

A: Tough Mudder was founded out of the desire not only to build an event where teamwork sits above all else, but to build a community that echoed those values. At the time of its inception there was nothing out there like Tough Mudder, in which people came together to complete a challenge where camaraderie and working together trumped finisher times and a "winner's first" mentality.

Our first event series—Tough Mudder—was a ten- to twelve-mile obstacle course designed by British Special Forces to challenge participants both physically and mentally. Before our very first event in 2010, we expected about five hundred people to attend, but in the end over five thousand people attended. I think we knew that our events would tap into a very specific set of values, but we underestimated just how successful we would be from the start.

As we continue to define ourselves more and more as a lifestyle brand, it's not just about our events; that would be too narrow of an approach to take. We reach people across several touch points, whether it's through social media, pre-event training opportunities, community happy hours, Facebook Livestream so you can tune in from wherever you are, and more.

Q: The social currency linked to Tough Mudder is undeniably strong. What makes your brand so shareable?

A: We set out six years ago to build a lifestyle brand and not solely an events company. Because of the nature of what we're doing, we give people a chance to be part of a story and a community of shared experiences. Today's customers seek experiences over luxury goods, and Tough Mudder is an experience that can unite people across the globe. For that reason, word-of-mouth may have been much easier for us than some other brands. Our participants are certainly entitled to bragging rights; that's simply part of what you earn by saying you've done a Tough Mudder and you're part of that tribe, and shareability comes naturally with that.

We nailed the word-of-mouth marketing fairly easy and early on, but it's a lot more work to grow the company into a lifestyle brand. We have to adopt new strategies, become fluent in all types of marketing channels, get smarter with data and consumer insights, and become more sophisticated with our product offerings in order to truly shift from a start-up to an evolved corporation, a lifestyle brand that people want to engage with every day.

The aspects of teamwork and camaraderie and the extreme mental and physical challenges that participants experience at our events are what make Tough Mudder truly unique, so we have something that people genuinely want to talk about with their friends or share on social media. For example, we make sure that all campaigns, no matter how big or small, express Tough Mudder core values and never put those values at risk. Across all our marketing channels, we always look to highlight our core values, some of which are teamwork, camaraderie, and triumph.

We are in the business of making memories at first-class events with signature obstacles. No matter what the platform, the key is conveying the message that Tough Mudder is more than an athletic challenge—it's a lifestyle. Those people who truly have made Tough Mudder a part of their lives want to share the experience with others.

Q: Arctic Enema. Firewalker. Electroshock Therapy. These names are not for the faint of heart. What is the core human need that these obstacles satiate?

A: Always irreverent in our approach, we consider being able to push the needle or "surprise and delight" customers a part of what we do. We've always taken on a unique perspective and voice as a brand, and it's worked in our favor because it's authentic and genuine to who we are.

More than 2.5 million people around the world know and love these obstacles and can say they've done something called Arctic Enema and Electroshock Therapy. It's not just about diving into ice-cold water or being shocked with ten thousand volts of electricity; it's about being part of something truly greater than yourself and overcoming obstacles as a team—and having an epic story to tell. People will always want experiences that push their physical or mental boundaries, and that core value will never go away. We are building a global tribe and starting a movement that unites people through the shared Tough Mudder experiences—people who live courage, personal accomplishment, and teamwork in their everyday lives.

Q: From a marketing perspective, if Tough Mudder could have a do-over what would it be?

A: When we launched the new event series, Tough Mudder Half, in 2010, I think we were a bit surprised by the reaction from some of our most loyal fans. Tough Mudder Half is a five-mile version of Tough Mudder that is designed to require less training and provide an accessible, yet rewarding challenge. It does not include the more daunting obstacles the full Tough Mudder is known for (like ones with ice and electricity). We launched it as a way to continue growing a global tribe and create an "entry point" into Tough Mudder. Some of the reactions told us that some fans thought Tough Mudder Half meant we were creating an "easier" or "watered-down" version.

In hindsight, I think we could have launched the event with a clearer message that Tough Mudder Half was intended for an entirely new audience and to bring more people into the global tribe. Our existing community is always asking for tougher challenges and more extreme obstacles, which we deliver by designing new events and obstacles for them. We knew that many people were interested in the full event, but for various reasons preferred a shorter-distance format, which is why we developed Tough Mudder Half. Looking back, we should have been more clear that Tough Mudder Half was an addition to the Tough Mudder family of brands, not a replacement. From a marketing perspective, the strategy, vision, and consumer insights we used to develop Tough Mudder Half were very strong. When you have a community of very vocal and passionate fans, you have to be prepared for their reaction to anything you do. It's not a bad problem to have, but it certainly requires you to always take a customer-first approach as a marketer and a brand.

WE'RE HERE TO (COMPULSIVELY) SERVE YOU

Be so good they can't ignore you.

STEVE MARTIN

I've said it before, and I'll say it again: being able to walk into Whole Foods and grab a piece of fruit out of their free fruit basket isn't just smart marketing—it's smart service that speaks to the company's higher purpose: delivering to the extent that it becomes the very definition of the brand.

The Whole Foods fruit basket is a prime manifestation of the compulsive servitude trait of empowered challengers.

So, what exactly *is* compulsive servitude? Does your brand have to hand out ripe pears to embody this trait? While that might get noticed, the answer is no.

Brands that have mastered the art of compulsively serving often start down that path by empowering their internal teams. If people who work at a company feel compelled to consistently go above and beyond customer expectations—and they're encouraged and enabled by the corporate culture throughout that process—overdelivery becomes not only *what they do* but also *who they are.*

Jimmy Johnson, the great football player, coach, and commentator, once said, "The difference between ordinary and extraordinary is that little bit of extra." Johnson knew how to deliver, too—he turned the Dallas Cowboys from a "one to fifteen" team to back-to-back champions in the early 1990s. It didn't happen quietly, though. The Cowboys made a powerful change when they hired Johnson, an operational change that became imbedded in their DNA and really drove the team to success. As a coach, Johnson insisted that his team deliver—even if that meant by doing nothing other than simply *trying harder* than their competitors.

Brands can learn something from that. Compulsive servitude can truly become the backbone of brand positioning if it becomes an operational goal. As an operational goal, though, that makes it inherently inward-facing, right? Not exactly. **You see, compulsive servitude done well starts internally but is expressed outwardly via the right communication strategy**. Then, brands can leverage that story in really powerful ways to reach their audiences.

Audiences respond to that, by the way. These are the FedEx patrons who now appreciate an entirely new and improved way to send things. They're the guests at the Ritz-Carltons who were granted requests they hadn't even thought to utter out loud, walking up to their rooms to find their favorite food or beverage waiting for them.

Now, wait—maybe you're thinking this last scenario actually *isn't* that remarkable. After all, the Ritz-Carlton *is* a luxury brand. While that's certainly true, it's a luxury brand that has incorporated a personal touch and doesn't take the loyalty of its customers for granted.

Not all companies excelling at compulsive servitude are luxury brands. Niche grocer Trader Joe's, for example, will open products right off the store shelves for people to try. Don't believe it? I didn't, either, until I had the following conversation with my mother:

Mom: "Have you tried the hazelnut almonds from Trader Joe's?"

Me: "No, I sure haven't."

Mom: "They're great. I just went in there and asked them to open up a bag so I could try them, and they did."

Me, flabbergasted: "So, wait. You can just walk up to the person working at Trader Joe's and ask them to rip open a package of banana chips or popcorn so you can have a taste?"

Mom: "Of course. They do it all the time for customers. I bought three bags."

Now, if I went into the big chain grocery store down the street and started asking the apron-clad employees to peel open a wheel of Brie cheese so I could have a nibble or three, I might be asked to leave. But in Trader Joe's? No problem.

It's not that Trader Joe's gives my mom snacks when she asks that's incredibly important here—*it's that she took the time to specifically tell me about it*. Have you ever heard the saying "Love begets love"? This is a classic example of brand advocacy as a product of implementing compulsive servitude—not just displaying good customer service, but empowering employees and creating a shareable culture around that operational belief.

Brands that aren't Goliaths need to differentiate themselves to earn this level of advocacy, and that means doing more than smiling when they answer the phone. They need a whole new level of customer service, one that's creative and ownable.

Do you know what brand is nailing that? UrbanStems. Recently, I was looking to send flowers to family members in Washington, DC. Naturally, I Googled my options for florists, and UrbanStems caught my attention. The website design was human and clean. Their reach seemed to be powered by share—another plus to someone in the advertising industry. From a typical purchasing standpoint, everything went smoothly—great selection, fair prices, nice user interface, and easy checkout. Wham bam. Case closed. Right?

Wrong.

In a matter of hours—yes, hours—I received an email from the company. It was an order confirmation like I'd never seen: a photograph of the exact flowers I ordered in the hands of the person delivering them. Oh, and the photo was taken outside my family members' front door.

Then, there was this note:

> *Hi Prentice.*
>
> *Thank you for using UrbanStems today. You're the best! I just want you to know your order was safely delivered and share a photo of the bouquet at its destination. Time to check off "make someone's day" from your to-do list. Have a lovely day, and we hope to see you soon.*
>
> *Lisa*

Now, I've ordered flowers my whole life, and this experience was unparalleled. I almost wanted to send flowers to random DC residents so I could get more smile-inducing emails from Lisa. That day, UrbanStems did more than deliver flowers to my family. They *over*delivered me, the sender, an experience as well, in the form of incredible customer service. It didn't take them a lot of time or money to add value to the experience, either—in fact, it took very little in that regard. What it did take was effort—that something extra Jimmy Johnson was talking about when he turned the Dallas Cowboys around.

Companies like the Ritz-Carlton, Trader Joe's, and

UrbanStems excel at compulsive servitude because they empower their staff to make good decisions. It's obvious when a company makes this effort. Take Nordstrom, for example. A few years ago, I was running down the street in my flip-flops—don't ask me why—and part of my shoe tore right off. Upon closer inspection, it appeared that my dog may have chewed on them just enough to cause the tear. Either way, the shoes were relatively new, and I'd gotten them from Nordstrom—so I just took them back and explained what happened. The salesperson didn't ask for my dog's alibi. He didn't debate with me or try to place blame. He didn't make the case that well-made, sturdy flip-flops don't just combust on the street.

Do you know what he *did* do, though? He went to the back, brought me out a new pair of flip-flops, and told me to have a great day. No questions asked. Now, to me, I consider that level of service simply the Nordstrom way, and smaller upstart brands could learn a lot just by spending a few hours in the Nordstrom shoe department, observing how compulsive servitude has set their brand apart.

When I left Nordstrom that day, I shared my story with friends. It's been some fifteen or so years after the incident, and I still shop at Nordstrom for all my shoes. I want to show my allegiance to them, and I want others to know why.

It's important for brands to take lessons from the UrbanStems and Nordstrom of today. It's not enough to greet customers with kindness and a smile—that's not only old-school, but it's table stakes. Still do them, of course, but those small actions aren't enough to differentiate.

I've talked at length about what happens when brands get customer service right, but what happens when they fail? What occurs when they don't effectively serve their customers?

It's called the Yelp effect, the scenario in which consumers have ultimate control. Just like a customer can determine a brand's place through sharing their brand loyalty or posting a positive tweet, they can also bring them to their knees by taking negative experiences to review sites such as Yelp. We're in an entirely new world of real-time customer feedback.

Here in Austin, we have a challenger brand that's reinventing the review space. Humm Systems created a platform that allows customer-experience-oriented businesses such as hospitals to get real-time feedback from customers via tablets and kiosks. Now, a clinic or an urgent-care facility can pop open a dashboard to see how well they are serving patients at any given moment. *That's* power to the people.

As I see how Humm is taking off, it's a reminder that customer feedback should not (and cannot) be swept under the rug. As your competitors raise the bar on their customer service, consumers are paying attention. What's the "so what" here? It means that new bar is now *your* bar. You have to treat your customers well and overdeliver, surprising and delighting them at every opportunity in ways that they'll be excited about sharing.

IS IT HOT IN HERE, OR IS THAT JUST RACKSPACE'S CUSTOMER SERVICE?

Let's dive a little deeper into a brand that not only believes in overdelivering—they've made it a client-facing promise. I'm talking about Rackspace, a cloud services company. They never had the resources to go toe-to-toe with Fortune 500 enterprises, but they did identify one area where they could make a name for themselves in the crowded cloud market: customer service.

In order to seize that opportunity, Rackspace created something called the Fanatical Support Promise. It revolves around five key elements of customer service: responsiveness, ownership, expertise, resourcefulness, and transparency. There appears to be plenty of buzzwords in that list, wouldn't you say? It seems that way on the surface, but it turns out to be a lot deeper than that.

This is a promise every Rackspace employee can recite on the streets, and they're constantly looking for ways to make those core beliefs—that set of five elements that represent their highest mission—less of a highlight reel and more of their status quo.

For example, the company of more than two thousand employees recognizes winning team members they call Rackers by awarding them straitjackets—yes, you read that correctly. The straitjacket award is highly coveted, representing those who "do whatever it takes to bring Fanatical Support to life." You can't stop the Rackers who have taken home the straitjacket—they'll do whatever it takes to deliver a customer support game so strong that it deserves its own arena. In fact, it can't be contained—hence the Straitjacket. Winning is a big deal within the company, and it speaks volumes to how committed—no pun intended—Rackspace is to customer assurance.

Now, Rackspace's Fanatical Support Promise and oddly charming system of awarding straitjackets for providing meaningful consumer support are textbook examples of compulsive servitude-esque moves. They've internalized the concept, making it part of their culture and even letting it define who they are as a company.

"

THE NEW BAR IS NOW YOUR BAR. YOU HAVE TO TREAT YOUR CUSTOMERS WELL AND OVER DELIVER, SURPRISING AND DELIGHTING THEM AT EVERY OPPORTUNITY IN WAYS THAT THEY'LL BE EXCITED ABOUT SHARING.

"

You don't have to be a multimillion-dollar company to execute on these principles of unapologetic overdelivery. Sure, Trader Joe's will give you a taste of its almonds—it's a smart move, and they have the budget to do it. What if you can't give out free samples all the time or pass straitjackets from cubicle to cubicle? That's okay. You can most definitely still embody the challenger spirit of compulsive servitude.

There's a quickie mart near the University of Texas campus here in Austin. It's a simple store that's done something simple to break the mold, to make a difference in the eyes of its shoppers. So what's the secret?

There's a sign in the shop that reads, "Don't see your favorite product? Tell me and I'll stock it."

That's it. But for them, that's enough. It works. Too often, those little moments of communication with our customers are overlooked or forgotten. This small, family-run store, though, is inviting conversation. Just like the Ritz-Carlton does on a grand scale, this establishment is making patrons feel valued. They're listening to them, asking them to be part of big-picture product-line conversations. It's such a small step, but that open model of communication deepens loyalty and keeps customers coming back.

BUT WHAT IF THE CUSTOMER IS WRONG?

It's important to note that exhibiting a true spirit of compulsive servitude doesn't have to be a touchy-feely process. It doesn't have to be a Lifetime movie where nothing ever goes wrong, the sun always shines, and the main character—or the customer, in this instance—is always right. Alamo Drafthouse knows that. The concept for the Austin-born brand is unique because you can get food and drinks while you're watching a film. There's more that's different, though—the brand has got attitude. It's got an over-the-top culture.

Alamo Drafthouse loves their customers, but it never said they were always right. Some brands have a "do anything to please a customer" policy, no matter how crazy a request or complaint might be. Alamo Drafthouse does the opposite, taking more of a "we are always right, but it's because we know what's best for you" approach. In one case, a manifestation of this approach turned into a viral video with more than 4.4 million hits on YouTube.

The video opens with the following:

"The Alamo Drafthouse has a simple rule: If you talk or text during a movie, we'll kick you out. Sometimes, that pisses some people off. Sometimes, that pisses the movie talker off. What follows is an actual voicemail a customer left us after being kicked out."

Then, the video cuts to an actual voicemail the company received from said ejected movie talker. The proceeding rant is epic, ridiculous, and highly entertaining.

Alamo Drafthouse plays that video before movies start rather than showing the traditional, canned "silence your phone" messaging like you'd see in most corporate theaters. And sure, their approach might be a little like that of a brand that fosters rejection, but it's also heavily rooted in a sort of reverse compulsive servitude.

You see, the founder of Alamo Drafthouse, Tim League, values the theatre experience more than ticket sales, and he doesn't care who knows it. Instead of trying to cater to everyone with cash in their pocket, they focus on moviegoers who appreciate cinema as much as Tim appreciates cinema. His "no talking, no texting" policy is a rule, not a suggestion, for a simple reason: he wouldn't want his movie interrupted by someone doing that, so he's not going to subject his customers to it, either. He's actually *better serving* the people in this theater who care about the movie by weeding out those who would rather tipsy text or play Candy Crush.

You can see from this example that compulsive servitude doesn't have to be cookie-cutter. There's no one right way to do it—as long as you think about serving with intention, you're already ahead of the pack. Think about compulsive servitude as an extension of your *why*. Why did you start this business? For Tim League of Alamo Drafthouse, it was to create a place for passionate moviegoers to convene and enjoy the art of cinema.

SERVING BY EMPOWERING

Another brand that champions compulsive servitude from the inside out is Cirrus Logic, a global audio-technology and semiconductor company. The field is very specialized, and they hire some of the best engineers in the world. For that reason, they take their compulsive servitude inward, focusing on treating their employees *and their families* exceptionally well.

Once, I visited the Cirrus Logic office on Valentine's Day for a client meeting. I was walking through the lobby, and I noticed tables and tables filled with roses, piles of cards, and other Valentine's Day-appropriate swag. I watched as employees came to sift through everything, some just looking and others happily walking off with a few items to take back to their desks. They would come down in handfuls before retreating back to work.

Why? Cirrus Logic provided all those nice Valentine's things for their staff so they'd have gifts to take home to their loved ones.

I was blown away. It was such a nice gesture, especially because they were making it not only about the people who worked there but about the families of those who worked there. That's compulsive servitude to your own people, yes, but it also speaks to a larger part of the brand's communication strategy and overall ethos. The inside reflects the outside, and it's no surprise that Cirrus Logic has been recognized time and time again as a top workplace by both the Great Place to Work Institute and *Fortune* magazine.

That's how Cirrus Logic serves. On a more accessible level, though, note that the operational story of overdelivery can also be expressed to the outside world through customer testimonials. Those testimonials don't have to be boring or dry, either. Take Paula Sala's highly awarded GEICO commercial, for example.

Don't know Paula Sala? That's the point. She offered up her testimonial to GEICO's service, but the delivery of her message is what has sticking power. In a thirty-second commercial, Sala told her story about being hit by a storm. Both her cars were underwater, and she had lost everything.

It was Sala's story, but she wasn't the only one telling it.

Beside her in her living room stood Don LaFontaine, dramatic voice-over deliverer extraordinaire. When Sala reports, "When the storm hit, both our cars were totally under water," LaFontaine repeats it into the microphone as if he were recording a film trailer. She ends the commercial by saying, "With GEICO, we had our check in two days." Then, LaFontaine, in his movie voice again, says: "Payback. This time, it's for real."

This was a great commercial for a number of reasons, but it was also an example of how GEICO used a testimonial about how they overdelivered in real life and turned it into something digestible and interesting to the masses, all the while staying true to their own quirky personality.

What can you learn from GEICO's example? You can't always hire Don LaFontaine. What you *can* do, though, is remember this: **just like you surprise and delight by overdelivering to your internal team or your external tribe, you should aim to surprise and delight with the way you tell that story.** That's how compulsive servitude can translate into a modern marketing message.

☆ CHALLENGE YOURSELF ☆

WHAT CAN YOU DO TO EMPOWER YOUR TEAM TO SERVE?

What are the ways you can overdeliver to the extent that it becomes the very definition of your brand? To help you make that discovery, draw out your customer journey on a whiteboard. Identify the key inflection points where the customer experience could be enhanced.

Note, too, that these inflection points aren't static. From the UrbanStems example, we know that one of the key inflection points was the moment the flowers got delivered. Typically, that's not a part of the process at all for someone who is purchasing flowers on the Internet. However, their unique process and commitment to overdelivery made it a relevant part of the customer journey by sharing it back to the purchaser.

Once you have your customer journey down, make a list of ten ideas for ways those key experiences could be more unique or ownable to your brand. Also, consider: How could you empower your staff to make the customer experience more memorable? Dig deep.

EMPOWERED CHALLENGER TAKEAWAYS

As we conclude this chapter, you must remember these three points:

1. Brands that embody compulsive servitude have dedicated themselves to service such that overdelivery becomes not only *what they do* but also *who they are.*

2. Brands that have mastered the art of compulsively serving often start down that path by empowering their internal teams.

3. Compulsive servitude doesn't have to be cookie-cutter, and the customer doesn't have to be always right. There's no one right way to do it—as long as you think about serving with intention, you're already ahead of the pack.

COMPULSIVE SERVITUDE

URBAN STEMS

Left: Ajay Kori, Co-Founder, UrbanStems
Right: Jeff Sheely, Co-Founder, UrbanStems

UrbanStems treats customer service like its job—oh, and it also delivers locally sourced, reasonably priced, responsibly grown flower arrangements, sometimes in under an hour. With branches in New York City, Baltimore, Philadelphia, and Washington, DC, the UrbanStems brand is defined by its penchant for overdelivering. As their website states, even their customer-service and sales-team members are referred to as "Flower Mavens, whose sole job is to help you make someone's day. Smiles guaranteed!" I agree. How do they do it? Below is my interview with Jeff Sheely, cofounder of UrbanStems.

Q: UrbanStems shook up a flower-delivery industry that didn't seem to be evolving. What opportunity did you see in the marketplace when you came up with the idea for your business?

A: It was personal experience that inspired us to start looking into the flower-delivery industry. After one too many frustrating and disappointing deliveries, we realized that this industry hasn't fundamentally evolved in decades and is full of inefficiencies, leading to five main issues with the traditional way of doing things:

1. **Quality:** With most orders going through online aggregators that outsource their fulfillment, your flowers travel through a disjointed supply chain full of middlemen and long stops in warehouses, leading to massive gaps in service and quality.

2. **High Costs/Spoilage:** Not only do florists have to run a brick-and-mortar business; they also have an average spoilage rate of up to 50 percent—all costs that they have to bake into their pricing.

3. **Accountability/Reliability:** The big flower companies outsource fulfillment and often ship through third-party carriers, which can take days. And not only that, but the delivery windows aren't clear, so you never know when your bouquet is going to show up or even what it's going to look like.

4. **Pricing:** Most flower companies advertise low prices and then tack on fees and high shipping costs later in the process, so you never actually pay what is advertised.

5. **Customer Service:** It turns out we weren't the only ones frustrated: the flower industry actually ranks last in customer satisfaction of e-commerce companies—a fact that becomes

very apparent on social media every year on Valentine's Day and Mother's Day.

Add it all up, and you see bouquets advertised for twenty dollars that end up costing closer to sixty to eighty dollars and that have highly variable quality, all with no transparency into when they'll actually arrive. It's not a very good system, to say the least.

Q: When I send flowers from UrbanStems, I'm emailed a personalized note from my flower-delivery person along with a photo of the arrangement held up in front of the recipient's front door. It always brings a smile to my face as it brings me into the delivery experience. It's also a form of surprise and delight that you don't often see in the service business. Describe what a great customer experience means to you.

A: Quite simply, the customer experience is the core of every decision we make at UrbanStems. From the thought and care that goes in to the bouquet designs and the clean and concise layout on our website, to the incredible customer care team and the photo confirmation, we strive to leave the customer feeling like they've truly made someone's day special. We believe that sending should be as fun as receiving, and it's all a part of the "Send Happy" message we want to spread.

Q: Customers have come to expect a high level of service from UrbanStems. How do you keep your team inspired to overdeliver?

A: Well, it helps that we're surrounded by flowers every day! But more seriously, my cofounder Ajay Kori and I actually built the foundation of the culture of the company before we even knew we were going to be selling flowers. So many people spend most of their waking lives at jobs where they aren't happy, and we believe that if you can provide an environment where you have smart, kind, ambitious people constantly growing and learning, it's a true competitive advantage for your business.

Not only that, but we truly believe that a great customer experience will win out every time, and the only way to provide that is with a team—from the flower designers to the customer-care team to our in-house couriers—that is passionate about going the extra mile to provide that experience.

Q: UrbanStems is going up against some heavy hitters that could potentially outmuscle with bigger service areas or lower prices. How do you continue to differentiate and grow your customer base?

A: To us, it keeps coming back to pushing the envelope in providing the best possible customer experience. If we continue to enable our customers to make someone they love feel special with a hand-delivered bouquet at a moment's notice, that's going to be hard to top—no matter how much money someone throws at it.

That's also why we are carefully selecting each new city we expand to and really engaging within those communities. We could pack our flowers in a box and ship them nationwide, but instead we look at each market uniquely and focus on creating the best experience for the people in that area. We believe that only happens with a physical presence in each city and a team on the ground that is truly a part of the community.

Q: What's the one thing you wish you had known when you launched UrbanStems?

A: You know, a lack of knowledge can actually serve you really well sometimes. If we had known half of the crazy things we'd see in this industry, I'm not sure where we would've ended up. Everyone we talked to who actually worked in floral told us very adamantly that this idea was crazy and would never work, so being naïve and stubborn enough to ignore that and figure it out anyway really served us well.

Q: If you could have one do-over, what would it be?

A: I honestly can't say I have any massive regrets, because we really believe in testing and iterating, and every choice we've made has led us to where we are today. That said, launching during a blizzard on Valentine's Week in 2014 might not have been our wisest moment—but we sure learned a lot!

EXTENDING INTO THE OTHER

If things are not failing, you are not innovating enough.

ELON MUSK

The fifth personality trait empowered challenger brands can leverage is a big one: constant evolution. It's a big one because, frankly, doing it well is a really big deal, allowing brands to remain category neutral while expanding into other markets with their credibility already established.

Take, for example, Virgin Group. The Richard Branson entity comprises more than four hundred companies now, but it hasn't always been that way. When he was starting out, he only had a couple of small businesses. His big breakout came in 1972 when he opened a chain of record stores, Virgin Records, which later became known as Virgin Megastores. From there, Virgin exploded (in a good way): Virgin Atlantic Airways and the Virgin Records music label in the eighties, Virgin Mobile in 1999, and the list goes on. There's even been Virgin Cola and Virgin Vodka. In 2004, he even started a space tourism company called Virgin Galactic. Through it all, the Virgin brand continues to transcend categories with high-quality products that deliver winning experiences.

There is absolutely nothing one-size-fits-all about Virgin. Instead, it's the definition of a "what's next" brand. But why? It's because they outinnovate. I recently read an Instagram post from a friend who had just flown Virgin for the first time. He posted a glowing review, but it wasn't the review that struck me—it was the photograph that accompanied it. The interior of the plane was lit up in pink and teal and purple, feeling more like a nightclub in Vegas than another humdrum element to a business trip. That's the kind of thing Virgin does—when nobody is looking, they reinvent the cabin light.

The secret is in their ability to move beyond what they know while securely holding on to what made them great in the first place. That's true of most challengers who have embraced the constant evolution trait: whether they're overdelivering on service, on craftsmanship, or on being so forward-thinking that it's exciting for consumers to try to dream up what they'll do next, that forward motion is in the company DNA.

Richard Branson once said, "My interest in life comes from setting myself huge, apparently unachievable challenges and trying to rise above them... From the perspective of wanting to live life to the full, I felt that I had to attempt it."

Thematically, that's what the constant evolution brand is all about—being so dedicated to something so specific, but doing so in a way that's applicable to other categories.

We've all heard Costner's *Field of Dreams* quip time and time again: "If you build it, they will come." For constant evolution brands, this isn't fiction. It's their reality. Why? When customers trust in a brand, they'll follow as the businesses they believe in logically extend into new markets. Especially when the brand is a known commodity, it generates enthusiasm and opportunities that wouldn't be there otherwise.

Virgin isn't the only company hitting constant evolution out of the park. Here's proof:

- **Apple.** There's this little company called Apple—you may have heard of them. Sure, Apple is a behemoth today. Dial the clock back to 1981, though, and take note of how they leveraged a constant evolution personality to topple giant after giant through the years. When they started with desktop computing, nobody would have guessed that in a matter of only years they'd be making mini computers that go around your wrist, allowing you to check your email, track your steps, and remind you to take dinner out of the oven. Apple is innovation manifested into a brand.

- **Shinola.** Recently, I signed up for Shinola's email newsletter. There I was, looking at this form that's asking me to check boxes for things that interest me. They were seemingly all over the map—men's collections, women's collections, watches, pets, journals, and more. I remember thinking, "How fascinating is it that they go from men's collections to watches to pets, and I don't even question it?" It's because I know the Detroit-based company has long been known for delivering quality craftsmanship and providing jobs in the heart of America's manufacturing birthplace. Their attention to detail is incredible, as is their enthusiasm for and commitment to keeping as much of the manufacturing and fabrication of their products in the United States. It's that commitment and enthusiasm for their mission that allows them to make bikes *and* journals *and* leather goods

"

WHEN CUSTOMERS TRUST IN A BRAND, THEY'LL FOLLOW AS THE BUSINESSES THEY BELIEVE IN LOGICALLY EXTEND INTO NEW MARKETS.

"

and turntables. It might seem like a stretch, but when you have that thread of craftsmanship and core values that defines the brand on a deeper level, that's where advocacy is born.

- **TOMS.** Known for its one-for-one model with shoes, TOMS didn't just quietly embrace philanthropy and a higher purpose—they made it their business model. For every pair of shoes bought, they donate a pair to someone in a developing country who needs them. Then, TOMS started making sunglasses, too, with that same one-for-one model. I remember the announcement clearly because Blake Mycoskie, their founder, teased it at the South by Southwest Conference in March 2011 before fully unveiling the concept a few short months later. It made so much sense to me then, and it still does today. They're building a cohort of philanthropy fashionistas—people who care about giving back but also truly value quality and fashionable apparel. It was a shoe company that has grown in ways we didn't necessarily see coming, but that didn't surprise us, either—that's the beauty of constant evolution.

Constant evolution is all about logical extensions of brands. What if The Life is Good Company, the New England-based clothing and accessories brand, started hosting executive workshops led by famous spiritual gurus? Would you be surprised? No, because their brand is grounded in the concept of optimism. In fact, it was started by a couple of fun-loving guys selling T-shirts out of the back of their van and staying true to a concept they really believed in: the power of positivity. They didn't do it to be cliché. They did it because they believed in it, and that made other people believe, too. Today, they've become a tribe with products in approximately thirty thousand retail stores across the United States and in thirty countries.

Two thousand miles south and twelve years later came another brand with a tribe that's committed enough to follow the brand wherever they decide to go next: Yeti. Yeti was started by two brothers out of Driftwood, Texas—a Hill Country town southwest of Austin. They created high-end coolers for those passionate about the outdoors. The coolers aren't just vessels that hold ice; they're approachable luxury items that people can get to treat themselves. Now, what if Yeti started selling tents, rain boots, or deer blinds built to withstand whatever Mother Nature can throw your way? Would that surprise you? It shouldn't. Even though Yeti started in the cooler business, they've created a brand engineered to extend into anything that delivers on their promise of "Built for the Wild," boldly moving into new products like tumblers and can koozies. That's the power of a strong brand, a foundation that sets up the pretense for instances when products change but quality does not.

A TALE OF TWO BRANDS: WHAT HAPPENS WHEN BUSINESSES TURN THEIR BACKS ON CONSTANT EVOLUTION?

Some brands like Virgin Group, Apple, Shinola, and TOMS are winning with constant evolution, but what happens when a brand takes the opposite course?

They get squashed. Like a raspberry under a work boot.

Take, for example, Jamba Juice. It used to be such a popular business with locations seemingly on every street corner. Everyone loved them. I'm not saying Jamba Juice is dead today, but it has certainly deteriorated. Why that is shouldn't surprise you. Look at bigger brands in that space, such as Starbucks and McDonald's, that were always looking over their shoulders, adopting challenger mindsets even though they were (and are) classified as giants. Recall that Starbucks has grown by innovating, by popping up those Stealth Starbucks and revamping their menu to include smoothies and teas. They even started something called Starbucks Evenings where participating stores offer wine and craft beer, savory small plates, and exclusive handcrafted adult beverages like an Espresso Cloud IPA. Even McDonald's recognized the appeal, adding simple smoothie options to its menu. Meanwhile, what has Jamba Juice done to retain mindshare?

And again we have Blockbuster, a company that just plain

ignored what the customer wanted. As a video-renting collective, we grew tired of schlepping the VHS tapes back to the store, and no amount of jawbreakers or Big League Chew at the checkout could make us change our minds. Instead of adding options, functionality, and convenience, Blockbuster just added more movie-theater-sized packages of Raisinettes to the candy bins and refused to rethink its brick-and-mortar-only status. Then, it lost out on acquiring Netflix—perhaps one of the biggest coulda-woulda-shoulda moments a brand can look back on.

Moral of the story: some companies will rest on their laurels. They'll get complacent. They won't find ways to evolve, to grow, to remain relevant. They won't dare push their marketing campaigns into uncharted waters. They're the opposite of businesses that are inventors at heart.

HOW TO TAP YOUR INNER INVENTOR

To pave the way for purposeful innovation, start by going back to brand positioning—back to that core statement that sums up *who you are* and *what you stand for* when everything else has been stripped away. With Shinola, the three things that come to my mind for their positioning is that they create jobs in our country, commit to unparalleled craftsmanship, and always deliver a consistent customer experience. I believe in that. I believe in them. So, in my eyes and in the eyes of a good number of other consumers out there, they're allowed to go make soccer balls or recliners or whatever else they've got coming down the pike. They've unlocked their "so what" and, in doing so, have opened so many doors.

Looking inward and pulling inspiration from your brand positioning exercise is one way to tap your inner inventor spirit, but you need to look outside as well. You need to know what's in store for your market. When I do brand positioning with clients here at Door Number 3, we complete a competitive analysis, examining competing and comparable companies, market indicators, and big-picture trends. It never fails to surprise me how many key executives, members of management, or other stakeholders at companies are *not* tracking those things. We present the competitive analysis, and it's often news to them.

Now, in all fairness, I understand resources are dictated by company size, time, and budgets. In the case of many empowered challenger brands, those cups aren't overflowing. Remember that you can have eyes on the prize without blinders. Even if you determine that constant evolution isn't one of the five personalities you want to be a cornerstone of your empowered challenger strategy, don't ignore it. It should always be thought of in some capacity, even if it's just for self-preservation. To challenge effectively, you must always look over the horizon.

☆ CHALLENGE YOURSELF ☆

WHAT'S YOUR CORE STRENGTH?

Pull out that ever-important brand positioning statement again. What is your core strength? TOMS has fashion and philanthropy. Apple has innovation. Virgin has the "what's next" factor. Yeti has durability. Whatever it is for your company, think about how you can turn that into something new. Now, write down five products or services completely unrelated to what you're doing now *that could offer the same consistent customer experience*. Lawn-care products? Child-care services? Sporting goods? Tires? Trash cans? Candy? Dig deep in this brainstorming session. Things might get crazy, maybe even a little weird. That means you're actually embracing the idea of constant evolution. That means you're doing it right. Even if 99 percent of what you come up with is ridiculous, there's going to be a gem or two in there that could inform where things are going. After you've papered the wall with sticky notes (remember, only one idea per sheet!), focus on what's working, and ignore the rest.

EMPOWERED CHALLENGER TAKEAWAYS

As we conclude this chapter, you must remember these three points:

1. Brands that embody constant evolution remain category neutral while expanding into other markets with their credibility already established.

2. When customers trust in your brand, they'll follow as the businesses they believe in logically extend into new markets. Especially when the brand is a known commodity, it generates enthusiasm and opportunities that wouldn't be there otherwise.

3. Constant evolution brands like Shinola and Apple, among others, are inventors at heart. Brands that forget to look around the corner, like Blockbuster and Jamba Juice, risk getting left behind.

CONSTANT EVOLUTION

SHINOLA

SHINOLA
DETROIT

Founded in 2011 in Detroit, Shinola is a luxury lifestyle brand that manufactures watches, bicycles, leather goods, and a host of other products. While the merchandise is varied, Shinola's reputation for adhering to quality craftsmanship and celebrating job creation in a city known for going bankrupt allows the brand to transcend effortlessly into different categories. As founder Tom Kartsotis once said, "If we were just making watches, we'd be very profitable. But we're diseased gamblers." Along with those watches, Shinola is selling something even bigger: by hatching the brand in Detroit, they're selling resilience. They're selling a comeback. They're selling the strength and possibility of American manufacturing. For these reasons and more, Shinola is the epitome of constant evolution. How'd they do it? Below is my interview with Tom Kartsotis of Shinola.

Q: Shinola is always innovating and evolving. We can't think of another company that sells watches, bikes, branded notebooks, jewelry, pet products, and now turntables. What is the narrative thread that holds this brand together?

A: There are two threads that tie all our products together.

At the core of what we are doing is job creation, so when we look at a new category, we ask ourselves whether this category can bring manufacturing jobs back to the places in America where jobs are needed.

The second thread is product quality and design. With everything we do we make certain that the products we make are designed within the tight design and quality boundaries that we have set for the brand. We have a beautiful story and created an enticing brand. Perhaps consumers will buy one of our products based on the story alone, but that alone does not lead to a sustainable business. At the end of the day, all successful consumer product businesses are predicated on the quality and design of the product itself. Whether you are talking about a restaurant, a movie, a watch, or a turntable, if the consumer experience is not positive with the product itself, you really won't have a sustainable business. So we focus on the stuff, and we make sure that it's well made while, at the same time, it fits into the narrative of the brand that is predicated on creating jobs where they are needed. Over time we envision this ethos to include other American cities whose core issue is a need for job creation.

Q: Shinola is a shining example of American hardship, resilience, and craftsmanship. How much does the personality of Detroit inform your business decisions and the types of products you will continue to add to the Shinola portfolio?

A: I wish I could say we had a plan in the initial creation of the brand.

Detroit was initially chosen as the place to locate because the initial strategy was simply to create one hundred jobs in a place that really needed them. We planned to make watches and sell them to other watch companies, not so much to create Shinola as a powerful, multiproduct category brand. It was both a philanthropic impulse and a desire to experience the sport of trying to create a business model that was, well, let's just say unlikely to return the fruits that doing something less complex and more proven would have brought us financially. We did it because it was hard. We have since learned that, in today's world, reputations and great brands are built by trying to do hard things well. At this moment we are trying to parlay this reality into a brand that can create an order of magnitude more jobs than we initially imagined.

Q: Shinola has been described as both "authentic" and "contrived." What's the secret to creating a new brand with instant "heritage brand" status?

A: Maybe the brand is both "authentic" and "contrived." Maybe it is contrived because we went to a city that we knew very little about, that many people had written off as dead or dying. Shortly thereafter it went bankrupt. We took an old shoe-polish brand that was known for the phrase, "You don't know shit from Shinola," and we are selling a quixotic range of consumer products that sell from $20 to $3,000 with no fear of going higher. I guess that can be called contrived. It can also be called a little nutty, which may just be part of this brand's charm.

Perhaps the authenticity comes from transparency. Since day one we have been quite communicative about the trials and tribulations of the effort. We are open as to how we are training all these workers. We tell the narrative about how we come up with names of some of our products—such as the Gomelsky—about some of the incredible stories of some lives we have impacted to the positive and about all aspects of this adventure. It's fun to show people who have followed us remotely, via press reports, the factory itself. When they come here, you can see it in their eyes. They get it, and they appreciate it by an order of magnitude more than an individual can ever understand without seeing the place.

Q: What's the one thing you wish you had known when you launched Shinola?

A: I can't think of anything I wish we would have known when we launched Shinola. If we would have known much at all, we would never have tried this, and we would have missed out on a tremendous amount of fun. And while this business is not yet profitable and is still unproven as a sustainable entity, I believe that we have brought a certain amount of laughs and hope to a city that really is amazing. And that city has given us a bear hug. And that love has inspired us to work harder and to invest more. And we believe we are just now at the beginning of something that can prove to be a very good thing in today's world.

CONCLUSION

Once upon a time, Matt Seiler found himself waiting tables in Portland, Maine, at his friend's pizza shop serving all-natural pizzas. The dishes were organic. The food was a priority, a point of pride. But the beverages? They included Pepsi and other sodas loaded with the opposite of organic ingredients.

Matt had an aha moment: *Let's make sodas that match the menu, beverages that taste good* and *that you can feel good about drinking.* It was at that moment that Maine Root Sodas was born.

Matt discovered his own root beer recipe and started serving it at the restaurant. People fell in love with the taste and the message. Then, he started serving it at other eating establishments in the city. Some local grocers found out about it and decided to carry Maine Root Sodas in their stores. Around the same time, Matt's brother, Mark, was living in Austin and was coming down off some big, highly profitable years in software sales. He'd moved around a lot and had great success but was getting burned out. After 9/11 happened, sales started to slow. Mark had just lost a close college friend, who actually passed away while traveling to come visit him. He felt as if it was a sign from the universe. At thirty-eight, he had an epiphany: was he going to be a less desirable fifty-year-old working in the software industry years from now? The industry was so cutthroat—miss your numbers, and you're out. Instead of waiting for that to happen, Mark hit the eject button on his own terms.

So, Mark decided to partner with his brother on the Maine Root Sodas business, flying from Austin to the East Coast in the middle of January. He had no safety net, and the risk that accompanies any new business venture was increased exponentially because they were early adopters to the craft beverage concept. In retrospect, it was perfect timing; in the moment, though, it was difficult. People were familiar with organic chicken and all-natural salad dressing, but soda? It was new.

Mark made sales calls. After a month, he'd learned all the reasons why businesses *wouldn't* want to carry the product. He returned to Austin and walked into Central Market with a bottle of his root beer in his hand. He spoke with a salesperson who informed him he'd need to speak with a gentleman named Rex, the one who ordered root beer for the store. Mark and Rex's exchange went something like this:

Rex: "Leave the root beer with my assistant. If I like it, you'll hear from me."

Mark: "Look, I've got a wife and three kids. You have to hear my pitch."

Rex: "If I like it, you'll hear from me."

Mark went back to his car and waited. Five minutes later, Rex called saying he wanted him to come back inside to talk. Soon, he was in. From there, the business took off. Mark's brother, Matt, relocated the business to Austin. Besides the organic, all-natural root beer with no high-fructose corn syrup, they added a ginger brew, a sarsaparilla, and a few other products to the lineup. Today, they have operations in both Maine and Austin, as well as twenty-five different flavors of soft drinks and lemonade that sell worldwide in over 7,500 locations including

Dubai, Hong Kong, and Scandinavia. They're Fair Trade Certified, using organic cane juice from Paraguay as the sweetener. That certification means farmers are paid a premium for the product because they employ ethical and environmentally friendly practices. The premium pay is distributed by an organization called Fair Trade USA, which helps invest in building schools in the communities where the actual farmers live and work.

Maine Root Sodas has more than a great product—they have a great mission, and they have a great story. Mark came to me and my team at Door Number 3 to help tighten that story when they were trying to gain distribution throughout the United States.

We created a campaign around *free-range root beer* as a nickname to describe the product to people who had no clue what organic craft soda was. At the time, it was a heretical endeavor—looking over the horizon, bringing them something they didn't even know they needed. Maine Root's audience needed a reference point. They knew what a free-range chicken was, and they knew what root beer was. Put them together, and that was our way of saying, "Look at this! It's created differently."

Then, we had fun with it.

We had pictures of Maine Root bottles free to roam in the wild in Acadia National Park and along the coastlines of Kennebunkport. We had fun, undercover breakout videos called "No Can Left Behind" where activists busted into what we called "corporate root beer" to free the cans out of cramped cages. We created music videos. One in particular included a young man playing an acoustic guitar, walking through the woods, and singing a song called "Bubbles of Injustice." He shed light on the inhumane manufacturing practices at the big, behemoth corporate root beer headquarters versus what Matt and Mark were doing at Maine Root—you know, liberating an industry. **Free-range root beer became more than a manifestation of their brand story—it became an understandable point of differentiation when they had conversations with distributors and customers.**

It worked, in part, because a good percentage of their early adopters were mad at Pepsi or Coke. They wanted an alternative. Retailers and restaurateurs were tired of being treated like crap. They craved a paradigm shift! If you're a mom-and-pop restaurant with only a few locations, you're just not going to get the same attention that a giant restaurant chain demands. You'll get pinched on margins and customer service. Maine Root changed all that by offering a product that allowed them to differentiate from their competition, all while enjoying more personalized customer service.

In short, Maine Root did everything right. They mixed the all-out hustle an empowered challenger needs with a healthy dose of risk-taking and bootstrapping. You'd see them at farmers' markets on Sundays pouring root beer. You'd see them at the Austin City Limits Music Festival every year, just as they have been for over a decade and running. They built advocacy around their brand by educating consumers—a practice especially important to heretical brands. Do you think Harry's had to educate anyone on the concept of affordable, well-made, mail-order razors after Dollar Shave Club did all the work? The Seiler brothers of Maine Root were the Dollar Shave Club of craft soda. They had to do all the work because there was nobody else to do it for them.

Note that it's just as important to call out what Maine Root *didn't* do. Matt and Mark never said, "Look at our healthy soda. Everyone should drink this soda all the time!" They never said that, because they always held firm in their tight position that soda is an indulgent drink, even if it *is* organic. There's a difference, though, between drinking a regular soda then running to refill your Big Gulp and drinking an organic Maine Root—the latter, clearly, is more satisfying.

Maine Root managed to create a strong and growing brand in the shadows of giants by doing things their own way, remaining true to their vision, and maintaining the empowered challenger mind-set they still embrace to this day. Why? Maine Root knows that the beverage category, like many out there, is too competitive for complacency. Today, in fact, big brands are paying attention. Pepsi has developed Stubborn Soda. Coke, of course, has Hansen's. They've both come in and spent a lot of money to aggressively push craft soda. Mark, though, says he is unfazed. Because Maine Root is already established with a strong fan base, the behemoths coming in and spending money to educate will only help build out his category. In true challenger spirit, though, he'll continue to keep a tight grip on his slingshot—always looking for new ways to differentiate, fascinate, and, most importantly, outthink his competition.

EMPOWERED CHALLENGER TAKEAWAYS

Are you feeling empowered yet? Are you ready to challenge industry giants with the fresh ideas and reinvigorated sense of brand purpose you've gleaned from heeding the lessons in this book? Here they are one more time:

1. **Embrace your challenger-ability.** This is big. And it's hard. Take a deep breath, and simply embrace your position and all the potential that comes with that. Being a challenger is actually an opportunity, not a setback. Take a look at the brands that have

gone from being challengers to being empowered challengers. See how they're growing and kicking ass. I don't think any of them would tell you that their challenger status was a burden or held them back—in fact, they'd likely say just the opposite. Recall how Taylor of EPIC Provisions, the Paleo protein-bar company, indicated being an empowered challenger actually allowed them to make decisions quickly and blaze their own path. Yes, the lack of resources can be a trade-off, but focus on what you can do instead of your perceived shortcomings.

2. **Craft a strong positioning statement.** Your brand positioning statement is your price of entry into the empowered challenger conversation. Without it, do not pass go. Do not collect $200. You can't even think about the five personalities I've discussed or how to apply them if you haven't nailed your positioning.

3. **Know your audience.** Too often, knowing your audience is overlooked. Your messaging can be perfect, but what if you're talking to the wrong people? Question your assumptions. Is your audience too broad? Your messaging too muddy? You don't have the resources or the bandwidth to say everything to everyone, so dial that in.

4. **Embody one or more personality traits**. You have five stones at your disposal at any time to pick up and throw—no, hurl with all your might—at your Goliaths: lighting rod, heretical, fostering rejection, compulsive servitude, and constant evolution.

Pick one. Pick three. Step back to your brand positioning, and choose the ones that embody the DNA of your brand. Then work those personalities into your brand ethos in a way that is entirely unique to your industry.

5. **Turn your customers into advocates.** Advocates build brands. Identify a blindingly clear value proposition, and deliver, focusing on what makes you different. Then, key in on being fascinating and wildly interesting at every touch point. Being boring is a luxury, and it's one you don't have as a challenger. Secondly, resist the temptation to be everything. Stay in your lane. Don't change your color palette every three months. There's an expectation around your brand, and consistency shows a lot about your ability to deliver something that's high quality—every time.

WHAT'S NEXT?

Toppling giants isn't child's play. It requires the power of belief consistent to your purpose and a toolbox filled with strategies to help you outthink rather than outspend. I'm not going to sugarcoat the process by saying it's easy, either. It's not my job to pat brands on the back for mediocrity or commiserate with them about advertising budgets that are down. Rather, it's my job to ignite them. To empower them. To inspire them to challenge and show them how, regardless of limitations.

Know that going toe-to-toe with industry giants *is* possible. Of course, there's a bit of adrenaline—and maybe even a little apprehension—that accompanies the thought of such massive forward motion and change. To get started on your journey, first *breathe*. Again, deeper this time. You'll take the path to changing the game and stealing market share one step at a time. The good news is you can be confident taking the journey because now you have a road map. It's in these stories of brands that have done it before, that have succeeded because they felt empowered to challenge.

Remember—you don't have to go it alone. Surround yourself with a support team of strategic thinkers and creative minds, nail your brand positioning, and dig into the principles from this book. Then, get ready to play ball with the big boys.

"

TOPPLING GIANTS ISN'T CHILD'S PLAY. IT REQUIRES THE POWER OF BELIEF CONSISTENT TO YOUR PURPOSE AND A TOOLBOX FILLED WITH STRATEGIES TO HELP YOU OUTTHINK RATHER THAN OUTSPEND.

"

ACKNOWLEDGMENTS

With special thanks to Natalie, Mom, Dad, Lindsey, Brooke, Jessica Burdg, Brad Kauffman, Kevin Murphy, Kathleen Pedersen, Michael Portman, Tom Kartsotis, Miki Agrawal, Jerome Hiquet, Jeff Sheely, Kristin Groos Richmond, Taylor Collins, Katie Forrest, Mark Seiler, Shauna Martin, Bart Cleveland, Blake Absher, Mark Killian, MP Mueller, Ruth Frederick, David Slayden, Don Sedei, Ross Myers, Entrepreneurs' Organization Forum 17, and the talented team at Door Number 3.

ABOUT THE AUTHOR

PRENTICE HOWE is the owner of Door Number 3, a brand development and integrated communications firm based in Austin, Texas. Prentice and his team at Door Number 3 work with rising brands that may not have the resources of their category leaders, but are positioned to change the game, build tribes, and steal market share. In house, the agency develops brand positioning, handles media planning and buying, and executes creative for all campaign elements and touch points.

For more insights, tools, interviews, and real-life examples of what it means to be an empowered challenger, check out TheEmpoweredChallenger.com.

Made in the USA
Coppell, TX
17 January 2025